ARTISTIC INTARSIA
PROJECTS

Sterling Publishing Co., Inc. New York
A Sterling/Tamos Book

A Sterling/Tamos Book

Sterling Publishing Co., Inc.
387 Park Avenue South, New York, NY 10016-8810

Tamos Books Inc.
300 Wales Avenue, Winnipeg, MB Canada R2M 2S9

10 9 8 7 6 5 4 3 2 1

Copyright © 2006 by Garnet Hall
Distributed in Canada by Sterling Publishing Co., Inc.
c/o Canadian Manda Group, 165 Dufferin Street, Toronto,
Ontario, Canada M6K 3H6
Distributed in the United Kingdom by GMC Distribution
Services
Castle Place, 166 High Street, Lewes, East Sussex,
England BN7 1XU
Distributed in Australia by Capricorn Link (Australia) Pty
Ltd. P.O. Box 704, Windsor, NSW 2756, Australia

Design S. Fraser
Photography John Woodward, Stoughton, Saskatchewan

Library and Archives Canada Cataloguing in Publication Data

Hall, Garnet, 1949-
    Artistic intarsia projects / Garnet Hall.
  Includes index.
"A Sterling/Tamos book".
  ISBN 1-895569-69-9
    1. Marquetry--Technique. I.Title.
TT192.H342 2005   745.51'2   C2005-906453-6

Tamos Books Inc. acknowledges the financial support of
the Government of Canada through the Book Publishing
Development Program (BPIDP) for our publishing
activities.

Printed in China
All Rights Reserved

ISBN-13: 978-1-895569-69-8
ISBN-10: 1-895569-69-9

For information about custom editions, special sales,
premium and corporate purchases, please contact Sterling
Special Sales Department at 800-805-5489 or
specialsales@sterlingpub.com.

Contents

Projects

Introduction

After years and years of crafting I still find intarsia to be the most rewarding wood art form. Its latitude for creative expression never ceases to amaze me. I think of it as painting with wood. The wood is my pallet and I use it to create the pictures I like – from two-dimensional scenes and figures to stand-alone sculptured objects. What began as a hobby has now consumed my life and taken me to places, both artistically and geographically, that I never dreamed about. I have traveled across North America and Europe representing my art and demonstrating my techniques. I have met amazing wood artists and gained insights into the fine work accomplished in small woodshops across the land. It's a pleasure to share ideas with these people and find solutions to problems that help to advance the art of intarsia.

To date I have taught 800 students in intarsia classes, given over 200 seminars, and spoken to over 4000 intarsia enthusiasts. I have published two books, The Art of Intarsia and Creative Intarsia Projects, and written articles for The Canadian Woodworker, Creative Woodworks and Crafts, Scroll Saw Workshop, and the British magazine, Practical Woodworking. Woodworkers talk to me about their work and offer suggestions about projects and show me other interpretations of my intarsia patterns. Often a different choice of wood, a unique way to shape the pieces, or an imaginative use of a finish gives the project an entirely new perspective. Woodworkers bring me pictures of their work which I post on my web page to give others the opportunity to see different ways of approaching projects as well as a chance to communicate with other hobbyists. It's a learning experience for all of us. I invite you to see web site www.sawbird.com or e-mail me at intarsia@sawbird.com.

One of the most appealing aspects about intarsia crafting is that you don't need to invest in a vast array of expensive tools or have a large work space. Mainly tools to cut and sand are needed and you can start out with a coping saw and sandpaper, adding other tools as you make your work more specialized and complex. Prepare a corner of your basement or garage as your working area. Intarsia work is a learning process and you will discover new ways of doing things as you progress. This book offers a variety of new projects that allows you to explore different techniques as you work through the various ideas. As I have progressed I pass my discoveries on to you. For example, I now prefer a different cutting blade and I use another finish. These changes have been the result of continuous experiments that I hope you will explore as well. There are traditional projects in the book as well as unique forms. As we all contribute on skill and imaginative ideas we can take the art of intarsia to new and exciting levels.

This tiger head has the look of relief carving. The realistic effect is achieved by using varying thicknesses of wood — in this case ten — to enhance the perspective. Creative shaping adds to the artistry.

Getting Started

If you are unfamiliar with intarsia work you may wish to attempt a small project before proceeding to a larger object. I chose a daisy to take you through all the steps you will need. Daisies have beautiful curved petals and offer the opportunity to do some creative work. The pattern in this book (p26) is not too difficult and offers a special opportunity for interesting shaping. It is a popular project for men and women crafters. If you make several practice daisies you can make each one different. Use various shades of wood, shape them differently, and use different finishes on each (photos 1&5).

Choosing the Wood

Try to think of wood as your palette (photo 2). Instead of paints, however, the intarsia artist uses different colors, shades, and textures of wood to create the pictures. The choice of wood allows you to be uniquely creative. So it is important to learn about the wide range of wood available. As you evaluate each piece you will see it in the context of a particular intarsia project, and as you experiment with color and grain you will discover the many different effects that can be achieved.

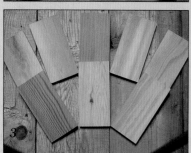

The most common wood used for intarsia projects is western red cedar (photo 3). It has the greatest variety of shades and grain textures and it is a softwood that's easy to cut and shape. It's also fairly easy to find and not too expensive. It grows on the western side of the North American continent from Alaska, British Columbia, Yukon, and Alberta to Washington state, Oregon, Montana, and northern California. Other varieties of cedar grow in different areas but none has the color variety of western red cedar. It is sold by stores that specialize in material for decks and fences. It's very popular in western North America but harder to find in the east, although lumber yards will order it. This wood offers all shades of brown that suit most intarsia patterns. **Note** In this book WRC refers to western red cedar.

There are many other shades, colors, and textures (photo 4) of wood at your disposal. Try to choose a variety of shades and textures for the most striking effects in your woodworking projects. For example, you can choose a variety of shades of one wood or several different woods and arrange them for the greatest effect. You can contrast dark woods with light woods. The choice is yours and it affects the final look of the project. See photo 5 for examples of different wood choices.

Working with Patterns

The pattern is your guide and should give suggestions for wood shade or species, which pieces to raise or lower, and an arrow indicating grain direction. Usually, the pattern will need to be enlarged if you want to make it the same size as the original (you can make it any size you like). For the original size follow this formula for the percentage of enlargement: original width divided by the width of the project in the book x 100 = the enlargement percentage. The size of the original project is given at the beginning of each project.

Transferring Patterns to Wood

These are three commonly used methods to transfer the pattern to the wood.

Method 1 Lay the pattern on the wood to take advantage of the grain and color. Place a piece of carbon paper under the pattern and trace the piece onto the wood

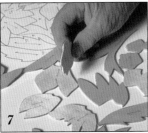

(photo 6). Good commercial patterns are printed on a see-through paper to help you judge how the wood will look for each piece.

Note This method requires that you trace very carefully. Careless tracing will result in errors that will impact how well the pieces fit.

Method 2 Transfer the entire pattern to a thin material such as ⅛ in baltic birch or MDF (Medium Density Fiber) board (photo 7). You can trace on the wood with carbon paper but a quicker way is to attach the pattern to the wood (photo 8) with spray glue or glue stick and cut out the wood to make a template. I prefer this method. The template pieces give a firm edge to trace around for a better fit. Also, the template can be used over and over again. One drawback is the time it takes to make the template, but to me the benefits outweigh the time spent. If you make the template from acrylic (photo 9), an added benefit is that you can see the wood through the clear plastic (often called acrylic).

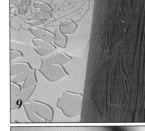

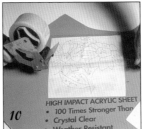

Note Purchase ⅛ in acrylic that has paper on both sides. One problem is that as you cut, the friction heats the blade and melts the plastic, closing the cut behind the blade. You could cut forever. You can slow the saw down to reduce friction. I cut with a skip tooth or hook tooth blade and have never encountered any problems, even using a #3 or #5 blade and cutting fairly fast. If you cover the top of the acrylic with packing tape (photo 10) you can cut with almost any blade. Once the template is made, lay it on the wood and trace around it (photo 11). Use a sharp pencil or pen and hold it at a 45° angle. Laying the template pieces out on the wood has the advantage of allowing you to get maximum use of the material.

Don't overlook other possibilities, such as slabs of man-made beam material, swirls around knots, unusual color variations, or different grain patterns to achieve certain effects. You can take advantage of inexpensive wood such as pine or spruce. Try combining natural wood, staining, and painting to create a unique style. However, it is interesting to note that most customers who purchase intarsia projects seem to prefer natural wood.

Wood Colors

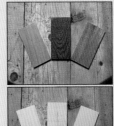

Black - black walnut, wenge, South American walnut

White - aspen, holly, basswood, spruce, pine. Use a clear water base finish to preserve the white color.

Red - bloodwood, padauk, aromatic cedar

Green - poplar, vera wood, staghorn sumac

Blue - spruce, occasionally pine (color results from spalting process). Use a clear water base finish to preserve the blue color.

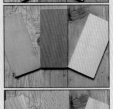

Brilliant color woods - pau amarillo, purpleheart

Special effect woods - zebra wood, bird's eye maples, spalted birch, spalted basswood, burls

Bottom left - beam material
Middle - spalted basswood and burl
Bottom right - different grain pattern

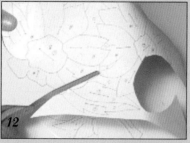

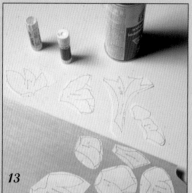

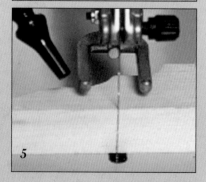

Method 3 A scroller's technique can be used instead of making a template and involves making a number of photocopies of the pattern, cutting out the pieces (photo 12), and attaching them to the intarsia wood with spray glue or glue sticks (photo 13). **Note** Some photocopiers have a small margin of error and all copies may not be exactly the same. So lay them on top of each other and make sure they are all the same before you cut, otherwise you will have a problem with the fit. To remove the paper, soak it with paint thinner to loosen the glue. You will need to remove the glue residue on the surface of the wood. Use paint thinner. The paper can also be removed with a heat gun or hair drier. The heat softens the glue, but you will still need to remove the glue residue with paint thinner.

Choose the method that works best for you.

Cutting is Important

Cutting accurately should be your goal. The more accurate you cut, the easier the fitting will be, making the entire experience more enjoyable. Practice is the secret here, but it is possible to eliminate the variables and give yourself a fair chance. These suggestions will help.

1 Reduce saw vibration as much as possible. It's difficult to cut with a saw that's bouncing around. Some saws are worse than others. Place the saw on an antivibration pad or use a piece of carpet or underlay. Then clamp the saw and pad to a solid table/stand.

2 Wax the saw table to allow wood to move and turn easier, with less resistance. There is a product called *Top Cote* for this purpose, but you could use furniture wax, bee's wax, car polish, etc. as long as it dries without an oily finish.

3 A magnifying lamp (photo 1) is helpful to follow intricate lines. Invest in a quality lamp that won't distort objects. You can also use a head band (photo 2) magnifier or something that attaches to a hat (photo 3).

4 A foot switch (photo 4) is useful for tight spots. You can stop the saw and still use both hands to hold down the work. Also if a blade breaks it's quicker to shut off the saw with a foot switch.

5 Hold downs are another option (photo 5) that come with saws. They hold the work down

and reduce the chatter. One drawback is that they impair the ability to see the line and move one's hands to new positions to turn the wood.

6 Some saws have a large blade hole in the table. Small pieces fall through and can go missing. It is worthwhile to make a false table (photo 6) with a smaller hole. Use $1/2$ in material. It will raise your work to a new area on the blade and allow more use from the blade. Varnish this top and then give it a waxing so it's very smooth (photo 7).

7 Choose the proper blade. Smaller blades require an

experienced operator. For a soft wood such as western red cedar, the 3 best blade sizes are #5, #7, #9. The 3-teeth styles to consider are regular, double, or skip. I would suggest starting with a #7 double tooth/non-reverse. This blade will not cut too fast and the non-reverse blades will hop less than a reverse blade. After a bit of practice you can move to the double tooth/reverse blade, then the skip tooth/reverse, and finally to a hook tooth blade which is the fastest cutter. The idea is to get good, then fast. At some point in this process you may find a blade you really like that cuts accurately. Stay with that blade. When you first cut hardwoods I recommend using a blade one size larger with fewer teeth per inch – #9 skip tooth, for example. Everyone has their favorite blades. You will have to discover yours.

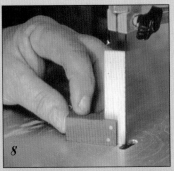

8 Install the blade with the teeth facing the front of the saw and pointing downward. It's difficult to see the teeth on very small blades so run your finger up the blade. If the teeth are pointing down it should feel rough as you move your finger up the blade and smooth going down. Take note of the reverse teeth. They can fool you sometimes.

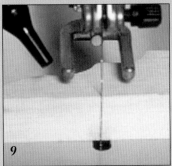

9 Make sure the blade is square to the table (photo 8). To check, make a kerf with the blade (photo 9), turn the saw off, and turn the piece of wood around but don't lift it off the table. The back of the blade must fit into the kerf, otherwise adjust the table (photo 10).

10 Check the tension. If the blade is too tight you may break a lot of blades. If the blade wanders it may be too loose. Holding the blade at the mid point it should move about $1/8$ in sideways with reasonable pressure. If you are a perfectionist use a guitar tuner. The blade is like a wire under tension and it will ring like a guitar string. I tighten mine to a "G", then pluck the blade every time you tension it and you will soon recognize the sound (photo 11).

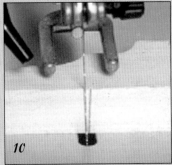

11 A reverse tooth blade has 4 to 6 teeth on the bottom of the blade that face upward. These teeth will clean up tear-out and save some sanding work. When using a reverse tooth blade make sure the teeth enter the wood on the upstroke. At least 2 to 3 teeth should be in the wood. Bring the saw to the top of the upstroke and look along the top of the table to make sure. Reverse tooth blades (photo 12) cause the wood to hop more so more pressure has to be applied to hold the wood down as you cut. The hold-down will help (photo 9).

12 Rounding the back of the blade removes the sharp corner and the blade can make tighter turns and will last longer. Use a small stone, hold it on the corner while the saw is running, and slowly rotate the stone around the back of the blade.

13 Blade lubricant (photo 13) reduces friction on the blade, the blade doesn't get as hot, and it stays sharp longer. Pine, for example, has a lot of pitch, which won't stick to the blade as much if you use a lubricant. Try this experiment. Cut into a piece of oak, back the blade out, put some lubricant on the blade, and try the same cut. I'm sure you will feel the difference.

14 Correct posture will make cutting easier. Stand or sit straight so you are looking straight down the upper arm, not off to the side. Place arms (photo 14) at a comfortable angle. I like my arms at about a 15° angle. Keep the biggest part of the wood in your dominant hand and use the index finger of your other hand as a pivot point. **Note** Some people prefer to use their dominant hand as the pivot hand and if that feels more natural, do it that way (photo 15).

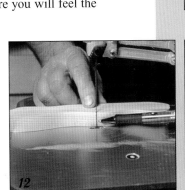

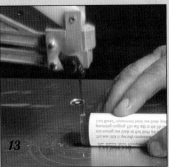

15 Align the pattern line with the upper arm and start cutting straight into the piece (photo 16).

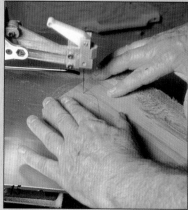

16 Saw speed should be moderate to start, then speed up as you become more comfortable with the saw and cutting. Slowly learn how to run your saw at full speed. It will cut better. Variable speed is a good feature. It will allow you to slow the saw down for tight turns, thinner materials, plastics, metal, and horn.

17 Feed rate is important. Don't push too hard or the blade will break or you will go off line. You will soon learn by the sound your saw makes how fast to cut. The feed rate will also affect the quality of the cut. A slower feed rate will generally give a smoother cut. Saw speed, feed rate, and blade size all interrelate.

18 I prefer to use the universal numbering system for blade size. Blade sizes start at 8/0 to 12, but since you are unlikely to ever see or find a 8/0, I will start with a 2/0.

   • The smaller the number, the smaller the blade, so the thinner the material it will cut efficiently.

   • The bigger the number, the bigger the blade, so the thicker the material it will cut efficiently.

   Here are some general guidelines:

#2/0 - veneers	#5 - $^3/_8$ in - $^1/_2$ in
#0 - average veneers - $^1/_{16}$ in	#7 - $^1/_2$ in - $^3/_4$ in
#1 - $^1/_8$ in - $^1/_4$ in	#9 - $^3/_4$ in - 1 in
#3 - $^1/_4$ in - $^3/_8$ in	#12 - 1 in - 2in

There are also blade sizes in even numbers. The thickness a blade can cut efficiently also depends on teeth style. The cutting speed of the different blade styles moves from slowest to fastest – regular tooth, spiral, double tooth, skip tooth, and the fastest hook tooth. The effect saw speed and feed rate have on the cutting process is explained in the following examples.

   • If you want to cut $^3/_4$ in pine, the suggested blade size is #7. But if you don't have this blade you could use a #5 and run the saw full speed and slow the feed rate. If all you have is a #9 you could slow the saw speed down and feed at a normal rate.

   • If you want to cut veneer and all you have is a #1, slow the saw and feed rate.

   • If you want to cut 2 in oak with a #3, you could cut it with the saw at full speed and slow feed rate. The blade will dull faster, but it will cut. This is an extreme example.

   • If you have only a #7 and you want to cut $^1/_8$ in material, slow the saw and feed rate down considerably. Thin wood cuts much faster than thick wood. It would be tricky to cut $^1/_8$ in material with a #7 hook tooth, but possible with a #7 regular tooth. As you can see, blade size, saw speed, and feed rate all play a role in efficient scrolling. Some hardwoods like cherry and purpleheart burn easily. Placing some packing tape over the pattern lines will help reduce friction. Using a blade lubricant and the packing tape will help eliminate this problem.

19 One of the hardest things to do with a scroll saw is to make a crisp corner. It takes practice but it can be done. As you approach the corner, stop cutting about $^1/_8$ in from the corner and allow the blade to catch up. While cutting, the blade is actually bent back, and when you stop, the tension in the blade will move it forward about $^1/_8$ in. As you make the turn, pivot around the blade and keep some pressure on the back of the blade by pulling the wood toward you as you turn the wood. This keeps the teeth out of the wood and they are less likely to grab the wood. Make the turn and line up the blade with the line and carry on down the line. This will make better corners. When first starting to scroll it's often easier to cut the corners in two passes. For an inside corner, cut into the corner, back out, and come in from the other side. Be sure to stop just before the corner or you will overcut. For outside corners, cut past the corner, come around, and start down the line again. Remember, practice makes perfect.

Cutting Corners

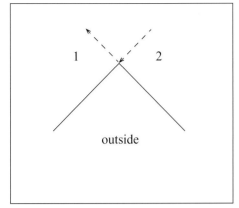

Cutting an outside corner
Cut past the corners as in cut#1. Then reenter the corner along cut#2.

Cutting an inside corner
Cut to the inside along cut#A. Don't overcut at the corner. Back out and reenter along cut#B. Slow down as you approach the corner so you don't overcut.

Accurate Fitting

Fitting is difficult and depends very much on how you cut out the project pieces. As your cutting skills improve so will the fit. Not many people can have a project fit right off the saw. You have only to be out a few thousands of an inch to affect the fit. Your only margin of error is a gap the thickness of a business card. So don't be discouraged if your first projects don't fit as tightly as needed. The more pieces a project has the more difficult it will be to fit, but you will improve as you practice. Before you begin cutting consider which of these techniques you will use to make the project fit.

Method 1 **Cut out all pieces, then fit**

Cut out all the pieces. Make sure your blade is square to the table. Start to assemble the pieces and identify any problem areas. A light box is useful at this point (photo 1). Look between the pieces and identify the problem. Mark these areas (photo 2). You can identify the problem areas by rocking the pieces as you hold them together or placing a piece of carbon paper between the pieces (photo 3) and moving one piece up and down to leave a carbon mark to identify the spot to be fixed (photo 4). Sand these areas with an oscillating spindle sander or set up a drum on your drill press (photos 5&6). A method I like to use is to hold the pieces tightly together and saw between the pieces where they meet. This method brings the pieces

International Intarsia Standards

Fitting can be the most tedious part of intarsia. There is always controversy about how tight the piece should fit. It's even a topic of debate about how intarsia should be shaped, or more specifically, how much shaping should be done. Whether it's acceptable to paint or stain wood or must intarsia be made out of natural woods is also a question. Some people even insist that intarsia must be made only from western red cedar. Others want to know what distinguishes intarsia from marquetry. There are many areas of controversy. As intarsia grows in popularity it would be helpful to have some answers and perhaps adopt some standards. International standards would be helpful for people who judge intarsia competitions and standards would settle debates about whether a work is intarsia or thick marquetry. These are my thoughts and I hope they stimulate discussion on the topic.

together nicely, but does require a steady hand with a scroll saw (photo 7). You must be careful when you use this technique. Continue to work through the project, fitting the pieces as you go.

Method 2 **Build the project**
With this method you build the project one piece at a time. Trace the common lines between pieces, as shown (photo 8). Then use the template piece to trace the rest of the pieces (photo 9). Then use the two pieces to trace common lines between them and a joining piece (photos 10&11). Continue in this manner. This method is a bit slower but will often yield better results when you are new to the craft.

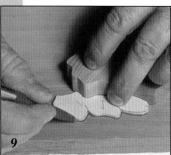
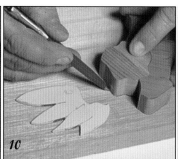

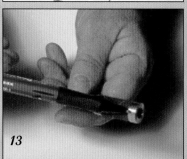

Method 3 **Cut pieces larger, sand down to line**
Cut the pieces a bit larger than the pattern, just outside the line and then sand down to the line with a spindle sander or drum sander mounted in a drill press (photos 5&6 p9). One problem with this method is fitting inside cuts or any tight spots. This needs careful attention. These areas must be cut on the line and then fitted.

Method 4 **Mirror Imaging for Accurate Fitting**
The Mirror Imaging System using Mirror Imaging Tools (MIT) developed by Gord Armstrong, is a method to create perfectly fitted intarsia or inlay projects. Gord's machinist background made spaces between pieces of an intarsia project intolerable to him and he designed a system to eliminate this. The system involves making a template by laminating a sheet of arborite (photo 12) onto $1/4$ in wood such as baltic birch. The bearings on the MIT (photo 13) run on the hard arborite material (photo 14). The pattern is traced or glued onto the template material and the template is cut out with a very small blade, such as 2/0 (regular, skip, or double tooth). I used a hook tooth blade. Do not use a spiral blade. Trace (p4) the template pieces onto the wood (photo 15) as indicated, but when cutting out be sure to cut outside the traced line (photo 16). Then attach the template pieces back on the cut out pieces (photo 17) and make sure the bearing is running on the arborite. Once milled (photo 18), the

pieces will fit perfectly. **Note** This technique creates a lot of dust. Use a drill press collector (photo 19) to solve this problem. This method is a refinement of method 3. It has one limitation. You still have to cut out small inside corners with a scroll saw.

You can try all of these methods and see which one works best for you. Once your cutting skills reach a proficient level the first method is the fastest. I now use the first method almost exclusively but I use the building method and even the sanding-to-line technique occasionally. Once you have experience with these techniques you will know better where and when to use them.

Before you start any fitting check the bottom of the pieces for splinters. You may have to sand these off (photo 20).

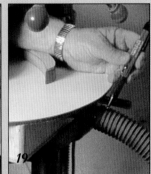

Generally, fitting can be frustrating. That's why careful cutting will make fitting much easier. Every project is different so it's difficult to identify one place to start. I usually begin in the middle of the project and work my way out to the edges, but sometimes I will do the hardest part first. Each pattern has a difficult section. The area is usually a collection of small irregularly shaped pieces. Patterns with large pieces with long smooth edges and few jagged edges are easiest to fit. Framed projects are more difficult to fit than free form pieces. I sometimes make the frame pieces on a project a bit longer or shorter to fit the project. Sometimes vibration can help to bring a project together. I have used my palm sander, held under the project, to set up a vibration. You will need a helper to hold the sander while you move the frame parts into place. Clamp two frame parts to the table forming an "L" and move the other two frame pieces in while someone holds a running palm sander under the table where the project sits. Almost everyone who does intarsia will have suggestions on where to start fitting.

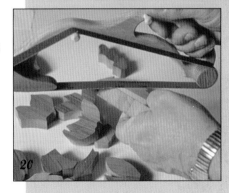

Use what works best for you.

What is a Tight Fit?

The pieces don't have to fit airtight, but spaces should not detract from the overall look of the piece. The shadow created by shaping will disguise small gaps. I like to use a credit card or a business card to gauge the width of the gap between pieces. If the gap between the pieces is no more than the width of a business card (photo 21) you are fine. A credit card (photo 22) width is the biggest gap you would like to see. The width of a saw kerf is another gauge. You don't want to fill gaps with splinters. This can

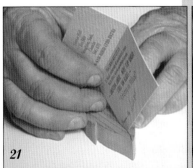

look unsightly. Neither do you want to paint the backing board black. With a proper fit the above two transgressions will not be necessary.

Note If you choose not to use a backing the pieces will have to fit tighter.

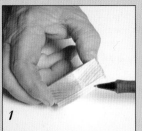

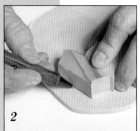

Raising and Lowering

Once the pieces fit properly, according to your standards, it's time to raise and lower pieces as the pattern instructs. Raising and lowering helps to achieve the look of relief carving. The varying thicknesses of wood allow the intarsia artist to be especially creative in adding depth and perspective to a work. For example, the tiger project (p94) has ten different thicknesses of wood to enhance the perspective of the piece. The patterns in this book are raised and lowered in increments of $1/8$ in, except where otherwise indicated.

Raising

• To raise the pieces glue scrap plywood to the bottom of the pieces (photo 1) you are raising if the piece is in the center of a project. But if the piece you are raising is on the outside of the project it's best to raise the piece with wood the same shade as the project piece. Plywood in this case can look unsightly.

• There are a number of ways to make the raiser pieces. Trace around the piece onto the raiser material (photo 2) or use the template piece. Cut out on the inside of the line. You don't want the raiser piece to affect the fitting.

• I prefer to separate all the pieces that are to be raised the same amount, then contact glue all of them onto the raiser material (photo 3). Once the glue dries, I set my scroll saw table at 15° angle and cut out the pieces (photo 4). Cut where the piece meets the raiser material. You can sometimes raise whole sections at a time with one raiser board instead of one piece at a time. Before you begin, look the pattern over carefully to see if this can be done.

Lowering

• Lowering is the opposite process to raising. The patterns in this book lower in increments of $1/8$ in. You can resaw the pieces thinner with a band saw. I use a small movable fence (photo 5) to resaw intarsia pieces. A $3/8$ in skip tooth is adequate to resaw the small pieces for intarsia. If you use a band saw, be careful. Small pieces are difficult to handle. Smaller pieces can be resawn with a scroll saw (photo 6).

• You could also sand the pieces thinner (photo 7). This would create a lot of sawdust, so be sure to have good dust protection. A 4 in or 6 in belt sander works well for this but it is slower than resawing.

• To mark the pieces I want to lower I have a set of gauges (photo 8) that I made for this purpose. The gauges are $1/8$ in, $1/4$ in, and $1/2$ in thick, cut from plywood. I found this shape fits most pieces. I usually lower by cutting material off the bottom of the piece (photo 9) since I have chosen the top of the piece for color or shade and do not want to alter this. You could also use a scribing tool (photo 10). It is fairly easy to make a scribing tool (photos 11&12, shop-made scribing tool).

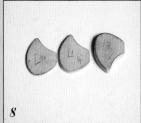

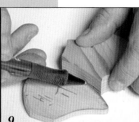

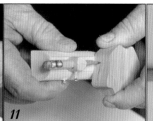

Reference lines

Once you have raised and lowered the required pieces, assemble the project and mark reference lines (photo 13). These lines will help you with the shaping, which is the next step.

Shaping

Shaping is another creative aspect of intarsia, probably as important as the woods you choose. You have to do more than just round off the edges. I have shaped three daisies in different styles so you can judge which looks best (photo 1).

When shaping, it is important to achieve a smooth transition from one level to the next, so that when you run your hand over the piece it should flow from one

Raising and Lowering Guide

	R	Raise $\frac{1}{8}$ in
	R1	Raise $\frac{1}{4}$ in
	R2	Raise $\frac{3}{8}$ in
	R3	Raise $\frac{1}{2}$ in
	R4	Raise $\frac{5}{8}$ in
	L	Lower $\frac{1}{8}$ in
	L1	Lower $\frac{1}{4}$ in
	L2	Lower $\frac{3}{8}$ in
	L3	Lower $\frac{1}{2}$ in
	L4	Lower $\frac{5}{8}$ in

level to the next except where the design suggests leaving a squared edge. Almost any abrasive tool can be adapted to do the shaping. The most common are stationary belt sanders (photo 2), drum sanders (photo 3), pneumatic sanders (photo 4), and bow sanders. Pneumatic drums are the best because you can control the firmness. By letting some air out, the sander will form over the piece and leave a smooth transition shape. Solid drums and belt sanders are fine for removing material in a hurry, but they are not as good for the final steps. Small pneumatic sanders can be attached to a small motor (photo 5) with an adapter or in a flex shaft used in a carving motion (photo 6).

A power carver (photo 7) works exceptionally well with small sanders. The best power carver is the high torque model, with a maximum speed of 5,000 RPM. Small pneumatic sanders are rated to run no faster than 5,000 RPM. Most power carvers travel over 20,000 RPM, much too fast for small sanders. When you slow down these fast carvers they have no torque and just stop turning when any pressure is applied — and you have to apply some pressure in order to remove wood. Hand pieces for power carvers

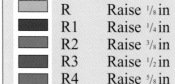

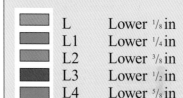

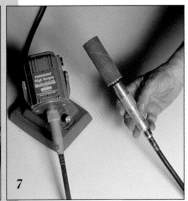

accept only ¹/₄ in shafted drums. The Sandstrom sander is a model of pneumatic sander with a ¹/₄ in shaft. A less expensive alternative is to use small pneumatic sanders in a flex shaft. The flex shaft can be attached to a small motor or used in a drill press or even a small hand drill that will turn at least 2,000 RPM.

A variety of small drums (photo 8) and shapers can be used in a power carver or flex shaft. These are useful for special shaping problems. Blue colored drums (photo 9) are especially useful for hardwood. They will remove material quickly but are so aggressive it's important to wear a glove on the hand that holds the wood. These drums leave a rough surface that must then be sanded smooth with a pneumatic drum.

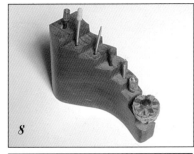

A sander such as the Sand-All Flex Sander (photo 10) can be useful in a number of situations. It's a nice complement for pneumatic sanders and allows control for detailed shaping or sanding. This is the only sander of this type that allows you to control the firmness of the

belt to form better contours (photo 11). Begin shaping at any spot and shape down to the reference lines (photos 12-14). The pieces should flow smoothly from one to another. My marking tool (p12) may help by showing where the guideline mark is for shaping. And the tool will mark different guidelines for different thicknesses of the intarsia pieces. **Note** This tool doesn't work well for very small pieces. Begin with 80-grit paper, then 120, and finish with 220. Pieces of the same thickness that touch each other, need only have the edges softened. Pieces can sometimes be shaped as a unit by attaching them to a piece of plywood with double sided tape and sanded together. This works well to achieve a smooth transition among a group of pieces. I am often asked about using a router for shaping. I don't recommend this. Routers leave the pieces looking too even and machine made. Another drawback is that some woods splinter easily using a router, especially on sharp corners. And finally, routing small pieces can be dangerous because small pieces are difficult to hold.

Sanding

After the pieces have been shaped it is necessary to sand them. This step is vital to give the project a polished professional look. You can also add some texture to the surface depending on what sanding method you choose.

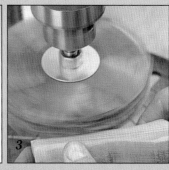

There are not many alternatives for sanding.

1 Hand sanding is one option (photo 1). Consider what works best for you. Sand every piece with 120-grit, then 180, and finally with 220. If you sand carefully with the grain at all times, you can skip the 180.

2 A flap sander is my favorite (photo 2). I have two, one with a 120 sleeve and the other with a 180 sleeve. The action of the flap sander seems to polish the wood and the 180 seems more than adequate for finish sanding. It feels to me to be equal to 220 that has been sanded by hand.

3 Another alternative is a star twister (photo 3). It is made up of alternating layers of sandpaper tightened on a shaft. I find it can be a bit too aggressive and can scratch the surface, requiring more sanding.

Texturing

It is possible to add texture to the surface of intarsia by using various tools to create some interesting effects.

1 Wire brush wheels (photo 1) can be used to texture the wood surface and leave it wavy by sanding away the soft part of the grain. This will give the appearance of hair. This technique is easier if you burn the wood surface (photo 2) with a small torch to further soften the soft part of the grain, making it easier to wire brush out. **Note**   Torching the wood should be done outside or on a fireproof surface.

2 Use a wood burning tool (photos 3) to add detail, shading, or special effects to the wood surface.

3 A fiber-burnishing wheel (photo 4) can burnish shading effects into the wood surface.

4 Sandblasting will give the same effect as the wire brush technique.

5 Leather stamps (photo 5) can add interesting texturing. Dampen the wood surface to leave a deeper impression.

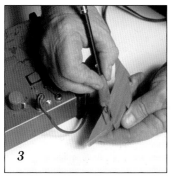

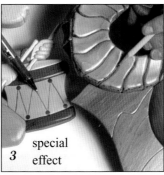

special
effect

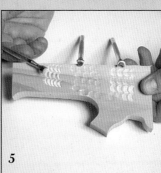

1

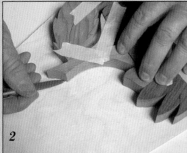

2

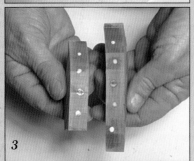

3

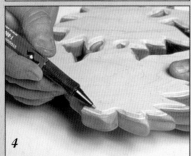

4

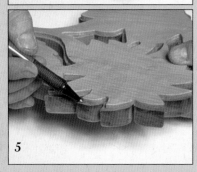

5

Backing

When the intarsia pieces are sanded smooth, it is time for the backing. Whether or not to use backing is an area of intense controversy. At this point it is your choice. The traditional method has been to use backing to help hold the project together but you can put a project together without a back. I will describe both methods so that you can choose whichever you prefer.

With Backing

1 I have found that the best material to use for backing is baltic birch plywood (Russian birch plywood is not as good). Baltic birch tends to stay flat, which is important. Certainly an ordinary soft-core plywood (oak or birch) will work as long as care is taken to keep it flat. MDF (Medium Density Fiber) board will also work. This material stays rigid and you can paint one side, which gives a nice looking finish.

2 The thickness of the backing depends on the size of the project. For projects approximately 10 in to 12 in square, $1/8$ in thickness is sufficient; for projects 18 in to 24 in use $1/4$ in; for projects 24 in to 36 in use $3/8$ in; and for larger pieces use up to $1/2$ in thickness backing. As a general rule the larger the project the thicker the backing. A backing too thin will cause the project to twist. A long thin project will require thicker backing for stability.

3 When you have selected backing material, assemble the project pieces onto the backing and trace around the assembly. Many people tell me that they have trouble holding the pieces together while tracing. This problem is solved if you tape the project together (photo 1) as it will appear when finished. I have had good luck by holding the piece firmly (photo 2) as I am tracing. An alternative is to edge glue (photo 3) the project pieces together with a glue gun or small amounts of regular white glue.

4 **Rounded back method** The back can be brought out to the edge of the project and rounded (photo 4) with a router bit or by sanding. With this method cut right on the line.

5 **Set back method** After you trace the intarsia pieces onto the backing, to set back (photo 5), draw another line about $1/8$ in inside that line (photo 6) and cut out on that line. This gives a raw edge which can look unsightly when the project is hanging on the wall. Some people paint this edge black to disguise it (photo 7).

6 When the backing is cut out, assemble the project onto it. Make sure it's evenly spaced, then begin the glue-up using an ordinary white carpenter's glue. Glue one piece at a time, set it back in place, making sure it is evenly in place. Then glue another piece and work your way through the project. On a large project I like to glue around the outside to form a frame that will hold the project together, then glue toward the center. I use a couple of compasses to pick pieces out as I go along. The glue has an open time of about 10 minutes to allow you to reposition pieces on the backing to make sure all pieces are evenly spaced.

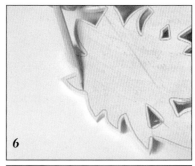

6

7 On small projects I prefer to spread the glue on the prepared backing and quickly set the pieces on it. Then I quickly reposition any pieces that are not exactly in place before the glue begins to set.

8 Another option is to glue the project pieces onto a square piece of backing. Then allow the glue to dry and set your scroll saw table at a 20° angle to cut around the

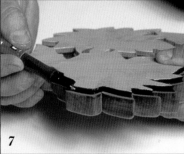

7

project (photo 8). This technique works best on smaller projects (less than 40 - 50 pieces that don't have many inside corners). The new Excalibur scroll saw is ideal for this type of cutting.

9 **Clamping** If the backing is kept flat, clamping the pieces while the glue dries should not be necessary. Just set the pieces in place and allow to dry. The exception may be the longer pieces on the edge of projects, although I have never had a piece fall out of a project because of glue failure.

With No Backing

I have created projects with no backing and find that it works well, especially on small items. However, the no-backing technique has been used successfully on large pieces by Ray Beauchesne, an excellent intarsia artist from Moose Jaw, Canada. Ray says that having no backing allows him to write the name of the wood species on the back of each piece used in the project. The project seems to remain stable. The pieces of a project made without a backing (photo 9) must fit very tightly together. You will need as much glue surface as possible. This technique works best for projects with long sweeping joints that offer a good glue joint. The shaping and sanding of the project will be the same as for projects with backing. If the project utilizes some very tiny pieces the glue surface will be reduced and this could cause a problem.

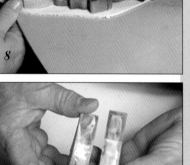

1 When all the pieces are shaped and sanded assemble the project on a flat surface. Place a sheet of paper or plastic under the project so that when the glue squeezes through, the pieces will not stick to the gluing surface. Begin the glue-up by placing the glue on the edge of the pieces (photo 10). Use ordinary white carpenter's glue. Use it moderately so it won't squeeze to the surface. Glue up the project one piece at a time.

Note Gluing around the outside to form a frame would not be a good idea here.

2 Allow the glue to dry overnight. Then turn the project over onto something soft (a piece of foam rubber) to protect the surface. Squeeze a filler type glue into the spaces, making sure it doesn't go through to the front surface. Allow to dry for 20 minutes and again fill any cracks where the glue has shrunk.

3 Sand the back smooth with a belt sander (photo 11) before the glue completely dries or use a thickness sander (photo 12). **Note** These sanders are easy to build from a kit.

4 You could also sand the back with an orbital sander 120-grit. The sawdust will mix with the glue and help fill any spaces. Now you can write the wood species on the back (photo 13). The project is ready for the finish (photo 14).

Hangers

Whether or not the project has backing you will need some way to hang it, Of the many different types of hangers, I prefer the saw tooth (photo 1).

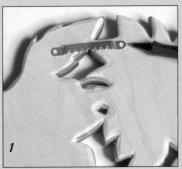

1 Find the center of gravity for the project. Hold it where you think the center is with your thumb and index finger (photo 2). Mark this spot with a pencil.

2 Use an awl to find the exact center (photo 3).

3 Attach the hanger in this spot or rout in the router hanger. Be sure the wood is thick enough in the area where you are going to rout.

4 To mark the hanging spot on the wall first tape a tack over the hanger (photo 4). Then move the project around until you find where it looks best and press it against the wall. The tack will leave a mark where you should nail a hook. It's best if you have two people for this.

Finishing

1 Any finish made for wood will work for intarsia. You can brush, spray, dip, wipe, or pour it on the project (photos 1&2). Most of my customers prefer a satin or low gloss finish and I believe a spray finish is easier to apply to get a good result. At least 3 coats on the front and one on the back are necessary, sanding between coats. Apply a finish after the glue-up in most cases.

2 Apply a gel-type finish to the pieces before the glue-up. If you apply the gel after glue-up the finish can get into the gaps and be hard to clean out.

3 When you want to preserve the color of certain woods such as aspen, which you want to be as white as possible, use a water base clear finish. All oil base finishes have an amber stain that turns white woods a pale yellow. Oil based finishes will brighten most woods.

4 You can apply the finish to the pieces and then glue-up, if you wish. One advantage of this method is that if you get some glue on the surface of a piece it's easier to wipe off and it won't soak into the wood.

I prefer to apply a finish after I glue up. It's easier and quicker. I like to brush on the first part of the finish and end with two coats of spray. I cut the first coat with 10 % thinner and apply it liberally by brush, letting it run into any spaces. When this coat has dried I sand with 120-grit and clean off the surface. Then I apply the second coat full strength, but sparingly. Brushing on this thin coat will leave fewer runs and brush marks. Sand with 220-grit and clean it off with a tack cloth or vacuum cleaner. Then I give one full strength coat to the back. When it's dry I spray at least 2 coats on the front, using the same brand and gloss as the first coats. You can apply a couple more coats if desired. To help with the spraying I made a lazy susan spray table which turns the project while I spray. Since spraying with cans can be expensive, this method saves spray and gives the same great finish at a lower cost. I hope someday to have a high volume low pressure spay system so I can try lacquer finishes.

Safety

Working safely is a great concern of mine. I urge you to follow tool safety instructions and read the manuals. Make sure electrical tools are grounded and in good repair. Keep blades sharp, replacing them when they become dull — dull blades cause accidents. When a blade gets dull it doesn't cut well, so the natural tendency is to push harder. This can lead to broken blades or cause hands to slip off the work piece into a blade. Never work when you are tired or distracted. When doing a repetitive cutting job, stop every hour and walk outside for 5 minutes to be more alert. Unplug a tool whenever you change blades or belts. Use push sticks (photo 1) for cutting small pieces on a table saw or other larger tools. The eraser end of a pencil works well when cutting small pieces with a band saw or scroll saw (photo 2).

The workshop itself can be a danger zone. Keep the work area clean and remove any tripping hazards. Make sure there is room to safely handle larger sheets of material. If not, cut them down to size outside. A good quality shop apron will keep your clothes clean (photo 3) and help prevent clothes becoming wrapped up in a tool (photo 4). To a large degree safety is common sense. If you have any doubts about what you are doing, stop and reevaluate how safe the process is.

The tools used in intarsia are safe, for the most part. A band saw requires more attention than a scroll saw. Remember that band saws are used to cut meat, so be careful. Scroll saws are less dangerous unless you drop one on your toe. But they do have a blade and a careless act can break the skin.

A broken blade will leave a sharp blade stub going up and down. A foot switch is a good investment to give you more immediate shut-off control of the saw in case something happens. Sanding tools can deliver a nasty abrasive burn and loose clothing can get caught up in spinning drums (photo 4) to cause some harm.

Dust Collection

The biggest concern in any kind of woodworking is wood dust. It is generated by the woodworking process. Intarsia creates a lot of fine wood dust. Take every precaution to limit your exposure to this dust.
• Protection starts with a good dust mask (photo 1) . The type with replaceable filters on the side and a soft rubber nose and mouth piece is essential. Disposable masks offer very little protection (photo 2).
• The next step is to remove all dust from the source. Every tool should be hooked up to a dust collector (photo 3). A small collector, 400-500 cfm is adequate for the tools used for intarsia. Blast gates at each tool would make the collector more effective. Placing it close to the tools is also important. An ideal situation would have one of these collectors for the sanding tools and one for the band saw and scroll saw.
• In this case bigger is better. If you want to collect from a planer, table saw, or chop saw you will need something in the range of 2000 cfm. There are some good books showing how to set up a dust collection system. Give thought to keeping runs as short as possible. Make the system as user friendly as possible and you will be more likely to use it. Have the system come on when you start the machine.

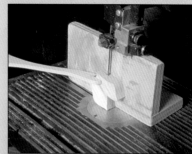

4

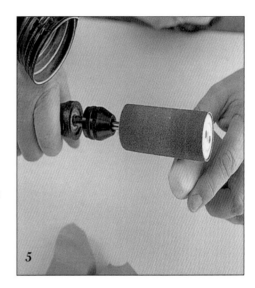

5

• For small shops there are some small collectors that you can move from tool to tool. One made by RazerTip (photo 4) can be hooked up to small stationary tools as well as placed by a tool to pull away dust.

• Small pneumatic sanders in flex shafts present a problem in collecting dust (photo 5). They turn in such a way that they throw dust toward you. I have devised a solution to the problem. My sanding station can be built by anyone. The plans are available on my web site: www.sawbird.com.

• Downdraft tables are easy and inexpensive to build. I have designed one that will hold a variety of sanding tools and confine the dust in one place It is an enclosed sanding cabinet (photo 6). The plans are available on my site www.sawbird.com

• The third line of defense is an AFD (Air Filtration Device). These collectors are designed to filter airborne dust. They hang near the ceiling in the center of the room or over a sanding area. They circulate the air a number of times per hour depending on their size. Purchase a variable speed model with a timer. The timer allows you to have it run for a hour or two after you leave the shop and over meal times.

• There are a number of things you can do to limit the amount of dust in your shop. Good housekeeping is at the top of the list. Daily clean-up reduces the amount of dust that can become airborne. One quick way to clean up is to vacuum the floor, turn on your dust collection system with a one hour timer, put on a good dust mask, blow off all the tools and surfaces with an air hose, then leave the shop. If you do this every day, your shop should be fairly dust free.

• It helps to clear off as many flat surfaces as possible. Have all hand tools in drawers or cabinets with doors, no open shelves. Remember that woodworking is a hobby, breathing isn't.

6

Projects and Patterns

Continued on p125

Variations of wood selection, shaping, and finishing for the following daisy project

Daisies

Shaping is an important element in giving any intarsia piece perspective and definition, wood choice is another. However, there are other special effects that can add realism and extend the scope of your project. *Carving* with a power rasp can add more detail and enhance the shape of the piece. A *wood burning* tool can shade areas for a more artistic look or add detail to specific elements such as bark on trees, animal claws and eyes, and leaf detail. *Wire brushing* is another technique to explore. This tool can give wood the appearance of hair on an animal's coat. *Stamping* can make interesting designs on soft woods and *sandblasting* is useful for texturing wood. Intarsia can combine a variety of skills and techniques to make your projects interesting and creative.

Daisies

If you are new to intarsia this project is a good one to start with and one that allows you to experiment. The pattern is fairly easy and it doesn't have too many pieces. The fitting is straightforward. The piece is quite beautiful and will look nice in any home. Make several daisies and use different shaping techniques to hone your skills. This project works well with or without a backing. It can be painted, although natural woods give it a richer appearance. My wood list includes a variety of choices in case you want to experiment.

No. of pieces   18
Finished size   9 $\frac{1}{4}$ in x 9 $\frac{1}{4}$ in

Wood needed choice		Quantities for each
Petals	Pau amarillo or oak or dark WRC	4 in x 8 in
Flower centers	Black walnut or pau amarillo or medium WRC	2 $\frac{1}{2}$ in x 4 in
Leaves	Sumac or cherry or light WRC	2 $\frac{1}{2}$ in x 9 in
Stem	Black walnut or mahogany or medium dark WRC (WRC = western red cedar)	4 in x 5 in

Directions

1   Enlarge the pattern (p26) to the size desired. Follow the formula on p4 to help enlarge the pattern to the size of the original if that is the size you want.
2   Choose the desired wood. I have given a number of alternatives. To me, hardwoods are my first choices. They give a project a richer look and make the project look artistic.
3   Transfer (p4) the pattern to the wood using whichever method you prefer.
4   A scroll saw is the best tool for cutting out the pieces. Begin with a sharp blade and make sure it's square to the table (p7). Refer to p7 for suggestions on blade size and style. Cut on the line or just inside the line if you are an experienced scroller.
5   This is a simple project, so the fitting is relatively easy. Take a bit more time and learn how to get a good fit. If you make a mistake and have to pitch the project you haven't lost too much. When you have all the pieces cut out, assemble them and check the fit. Refer to the section on fitting (p9) for tips and suggestions on how tight the pieces should fit.
6   Once you have a good fit, raise and lower (p12)any pieces the pattern suggests. Raising and lowering will add perspective to the project (photo 4).
7   Make a few of these and experiment with different shaping techniques. As in the photo try one with lots of shaping, one with little shaping, and one where the pieces are shaped to flow into each other. You can then compare and learn which

1

style you like best. This will also help you to see how important shaping is to a project and how creative this step is. It's possible to combine various techniques in one project. Assemble the project and mark the reference lines (p13). These will help with the shaping (p13). Shaping brings a project to life. I try to do as much shaping as possible. If you make a few daisies you can experiment with the shaping. See the photos of 3 different styles I have included for reference (photo 1).

8   Once the pieces are shaped, sand them to at least 220 grit. You can sand to a finer grit if you wish.

9   This is a good project to experiment with backing (p16). Make one without a backing for the experience. Refer to p17 for hints on a no backing project. To make the project with a backing, assemble the project on the backing material, trace around the pieces, remove the pieces, and cut out the back (photo 2 no backing, photo 3 with backing).

10   With a small project like this there is time to spread the glue on the backing board and then place the pieces onto the backing. The ordinary carpenter's glue gives you at least 10 minutes open time, which is enough to reposition a piece if necessary.

11   Once the glue has dried, round the back edges with a router or by sanding.

12   Apply the finish (p18) of your choice. Use at least 3 coats on the front and one on the back. Attach a hanger (p18).

	Pau Amarillo
	Black Walnut WRC
	Light WRC
	Medium Dark WRC

2

3

4

	L Lower $^1/_8$ in
	L1 Lower $^1/_4$ in
	No change

0

0

0

0

0

0

→ direction of wood grain

↝➤ slope down to this point

0 indicates open space

Chicken Kitchen Clock

Chicken Kitchen Clock

This project looks attractive and keeps the time as well. It is a popular gift item that is fun to do and fairly easy to make. It's ideal for any kitchen wall. Most of the intarsia techniques are straightforward. I used wood burning and carving to make the corn husks look more realistic.

No. of pieces 52
Finished size 16 in x 14 in

Wood needed	Quantites
Padauk	2 in x 6 in
Aspen	6 in x 6 in
Black walnut	2 in x 2 in
Poplar or sumac (green cast)	2 in x 6 in
Dark WRC	6 in x 8 in
Medium WRC	2 in x 6 in
Medium dark WRC	4 in x 8 in
Medium light WRC	4 in x 6 in
Light WRC	6 in x 8 in
Pale yellow cedar	4 in x 6 in
Pine	2 in x 4 in
Pau amarillo	1 in x 2 in

Plastic type clock movement inserts are usually inexpensive and easy to adapt to almost any design. They are available in a variety of shaft lengths to accommodate different thickness clock faces. You get a set of hands with each movement of your choice. The companies that sell clock movements also sell a variety of plastic letters. You can also indicate the hours with dowel inserts or wood buttons.

Directions

1   Enlarge the pattern (p30) to the desired size. Check the formula on p4 to help you size it to the original if you wish.
2   Choose the wood (p5) you would like to use or refer to the pattern suggestions. Begin with ³/₄ in thick material. The pattern suggests MLT and LT wood shades so look for two light shades of WRC with different grain patterns or some variation of coloring that distinguishes them. **Note**   Yc refers to a pale yellow color. Yellow cedar is a good shade but you can often find pine boards, especially ponderosa pine, with a pale yellow color as well.
3   Transfer (p4) the pattern to the wood with whichever method you prefer.
4   A scroll saw is the best tool for cutting the pieces. Begin with a sharp blade. Refer to p7 for blade choice. Make sure the blade is square to the table (p7). Cut carefully on the line. If you are an experienced scroller try cutting just inside the line for a better fit off the saw.
5   The difficult sections of this project are the rooster's head area and the corn cobs, chick, and leaves. These small pieces are usually the hardest to fit, so I like to fit them first, and then move to the rest of the rooster. Try this order. Cut out the clock face , fit the rooster's body, then the chick, corn cobs, and leaf area, and finally the hen. The eggs in the center of the clockface can be fitted at any point. You can get the eggs fitted to each other and then set the cluster on the clock face and trace around them. Then cut out the hole, cutting just inside the line. With a little sanding you will have a good fit. There is no right way or wrong way to do the fitting; these are just suggestions. When you have the pieces cut out assemble them and check for fit. Refer to the section on fitting (p9) for tips and suggestions on how tight the pieces should fit.
6   Once you have a good fit, raise and lower (p12) any pieces the pattern suggests. Raising

and lowering will add perspective to the project (photo 5).

7   The lines on the hen's feet are also burned in to add some detail. Assemble the project and mark the reference lines (p13). These will help with the shaping. The more shaping the better. I believe it adds realism to the project. Try to achieve a smooth transition from one level to the next. The section on shaping (p13) shows the tools used and the techniques of shaping. Use some carving on the corn husks. I burned in lines (photo 1), and then used a triangle file (photos 2 &3) to suggest kernels on the cobs.

8   Once the pieces are shaped, sand them to at least 220 grit. You can sand finer if you wish.

9   Assemble the pieces on a backing board (p16), trace around them, remove the pieces, and cut out the backing.

10   The letters on the clock are glued on. I use a dial face gauge I have made myself and marked the location of the hours with a light pencil. **Note**   The letters can be bought from any clock supplier. They are plastic and have an adhesive backing and are meant to stick to the surface. I have always used a dab of wood glue to make sure they stay in place. Glue the pieces onto the backing with carpenter's glue. Glue on the clock numbers.

11   Cut out the hole for the clock movement. You can use a large Forstner bit or a router (photo 4).

12   Apply the finish of your choice (p18). Whenever I finish a clock face I like to spray on a couple of coats first. This helps to hold the letters in place. Brushing on a finish sometimes removes the letters. You can finish with a brush or just continue with the spray can.

13   Attach a hanger (p18).

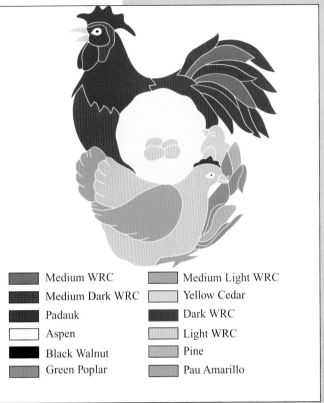

Medium WRC		Medium Light WRC	
Medium Dark WRC		Yellow Cedar	
Padauk		Dark WRC	
Aspen		Light WRC	
Black Walnut		Pine	
Green Poplar		Pau Amarillo	

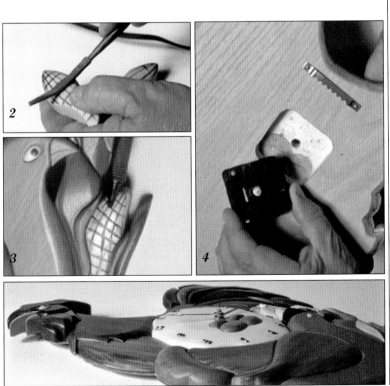

2

3

4

R Raise ¹/₈ in		L Lower ¹/₈ in	
R1 Raise ¹/₄ in		L1 Lower ¹/₄ in	
No Change		L2 Lower ³/₈ in	

direction of wood grain

slope down to this point

0   indicates open space
which is optional

Elf

Elf

This lounging fellow makes us all envious. But where could one find a mushroom big enough to lie under? This fun project is fairly easy to do and very popular with woodworkers. The mushroom looks realistic when you add dots to the cap using various colored dowels or small pieces left over from the woods used.

No. of Pieces   52
Finished size   16 in x 14 in

Wood needed	Quantites
Aspen	6 in x 16 in
Composite or medium light WRC	4 in x 12 in
Poplar or sumac	3 in x 6 in
Medium WRC	2 in x 6 in
Black walnut	2 in x 6 in
Light WRC	2 in x 4 in
Medium dark WRC	2 in x 6 in
Dark WRC	2 in x 6 in
Bloodwood or padauk	2 in x 4 in
Pau amarillo	2 in x 6 in

1

Directions

1   Enlarge the pattern (p34) to the size you desire. A formula on p4 will help size it to the original if you wish.

2   Choose the wood (p5)you like or refer to the pattern suggestions. Begin with ³/₄ in thick material with the exception of the mushroom cap. It's better to find some 1 ¹/₂ in thick material for the cap. If you use ³/₄ in material it requires such a thick raiser board it looks unsightly. The composite material I used is thicker than ³/₄ in. You can find this material in companies that manufacture floor joists or build mobile homes.

3   Transfer (p4)the pattern to the wood with whichever method you prefer.

4   Use a scroll saw for cutting out the pieces. Begin with a sharp blade. Refer to the section on cutting (p7) for blade choice. Make sure it's square to the table (p7). Cut carefully on the line. If you are an experienced scroller try cutting just inside the line for a better fit off the saw.

5   The fitting for this project can be a bit of a challenge. It's not too hard, but interesting. Fit the elf first, then the mushroom stem. Fit the ground area around the elf. The mushroom cap is easier. The flower is more difficult because of the small pieces. When the pieces are cut out, assemble them and then check for fit. Refer to the section on fitting (p9) for tips and suggestions on how tight the pieces should fit.

6   Raise and lower any pieces the pattern suggests. Raising and lowering (p12) will add perspective to the project.

7   Inlay the dowel pieces into the mushroom cap for the dots (photo 1). Use a variety of sizes from ³/₈ in to 1 in. Use different species of wood to add color.

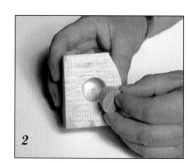

2

Note   Different colored dowels are available from a variety of sources. You can also stain some ordinary dowel material to get a similar effect. It's also possible to make dowels from boards. Cut the circles at a slight angle, about 5°. Cut outside the line (photo 2). The dowels will be a bit big and remain proud of the surface (photo 3) but it's easy to sand them down after you tap them into the holes (photo 4). If they are not perfectly round it won't matter. The wood will expand to fit them.

8   Round the mushroom cap, right down to the outside edge of the cap. You can also texture the elf's beard with a wire wheel tool. Shape the flower petals down to the center. Assemble the project and mark the reference lines (p13) to help with the shaping (p13). Spend time with this step to give the elf and mushroom character. You need to work at shaping the composite material to give the effect of the underside of a mushroom (photo 5)

9   When the pieces are shaped, sand them to at least 220 grit (p15).

10   Glue the mushroom cap first. You may have to clamp it until the glue dries. Then glue around the outside of the project. Assemble the pieces on backing material (p16). Trace around the pieces. Remove them and cut out the backing.

11   Assemble the pieces on the backing and start the glue-up. Use ordinary carpenter's glue.

12   When the glue has dried, round the back edges.

13   Apply the finish (p18) of your choice. Use at least 3 coats on the front and one on the back.

14   Attach a hanger (photo 6).

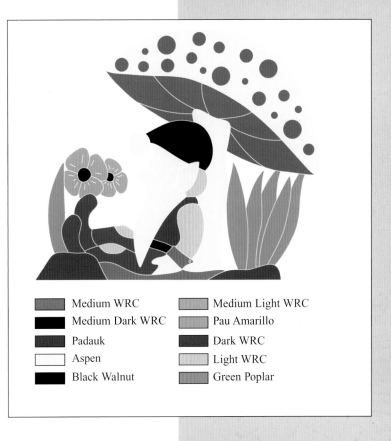

	Medium WRC			Medium Light WRC
	Medium Dark WRC			Pau Amarillo
	Padauk			Dark WRC
	Aspen			Light WRC
	Black Walnut			Green Poplar

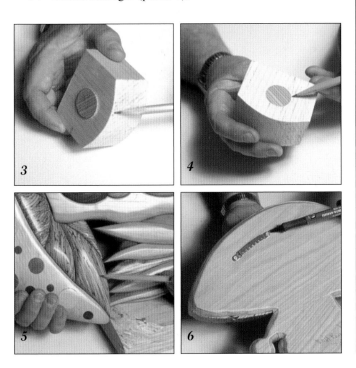

3

4

5

6

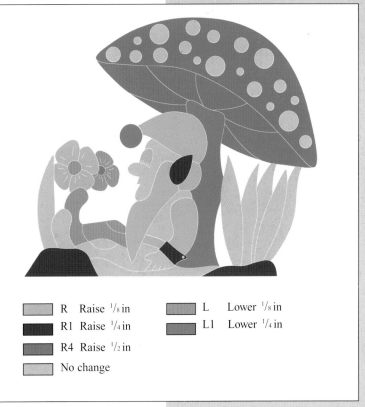

	R Raise ¹/₈ in			L Lower ¹/₈ in
	R1 Raise ¹/₄ in			L1 Lower ¹/₄ in
	R4 Raise ¹/₂ in			
	No change			

⌐⟶ direction of wood grain

⟍·····► slope down to this point

0 indicates open space

Fat Truck

Fat Truck

This is my version of an abstract truck. It's meant to be a fun piece and doesn't represent any particular model or make. I had a great time with the shaping. Each design can be different and unusual. I burned tread marks on the tires to give my fat truck a look of realism.

No. of pieces   48
Finished size   21 ½ in x 8 in

Wood needed	Quantities
Dark WRC	6 in x 12 in
Medium dark WRC	6 in x 12 in
Medium WRC	4 in x 8 in
Light WRC	4 in x 6 in
Black walnut	4 in x 8 in

1

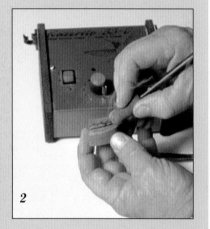

2

Directions

1 Enlarge (p4) the pattern (p37) to the desired size.

2 Choose the wood you like (p5) or refer to the pattern suggestions and begin with $^3/_4$ in thick material.

3 Transfer the pattern to the wood by any method explained on p4.

4 A scroll saw is the best tool to cut out the pieces. Make sure you have a sharp blade and that it is square to the table. Refer to p7 for blade choice. Cut on the line or just inside the line if you are an experienced scroller.

5 When you have the pieces cut out, assemble them and check for fit. Refer to p9 for tips and suggestions on fitting. I like to fit all the small parts around the cab and then work to the back and front in order. This is fairly easy to fit.

6 Raise and lower any pieces the pattern suggests. Raising and lowering will add perspective to the project. See photo 1.

7 Assemble the pieces and mark the reference lines (p13) to help with the shaping. I spend a lot of time with shaping to get the look I want, especially with this project which depends on shaping for its unique look. Try to achieve an exaggerated look by making the pieces look big and puffy. Burn (p15) tread marks on the tires at this point (photo 2). The truck is abstract so you have some latitude with shaping.

8 After shaping, sand all the pieces to at least 220 grit (p15).

9 Assemble the pieces on backing board (p16) and trace around the pieces, remove them, and cut out the back. Glue the pieces on the backboard with ordinary carpenter's glue.

10 Apply the finish of your choice (p18). Use at least 3 coats on the front and one on the back.

11 Attach a hanger (p6).

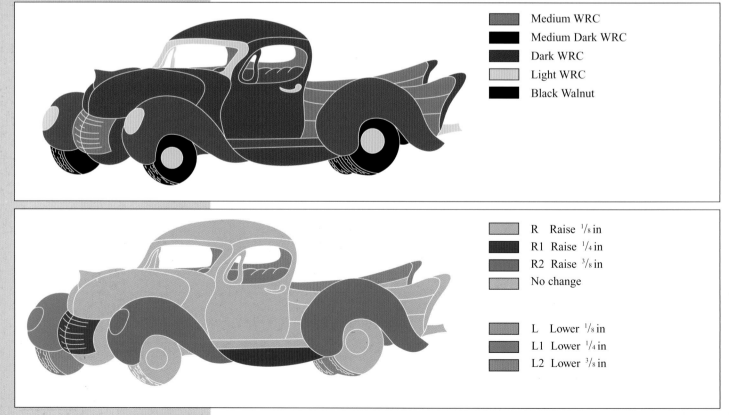

Medium WRC	
Medium Dark WRC	
Dark WRC	
Light WRC	
Black Walnut	

R	Raise $^1/_8$ in
R1	Raise $^1/_4$ in
R2	Raise $^3/_8$ in
	No change
L	Lower $^1/_8$ in
L1	Lower $^1/_4$ in
L2	Lower $^3/_8$ in

Pattern 40% original size

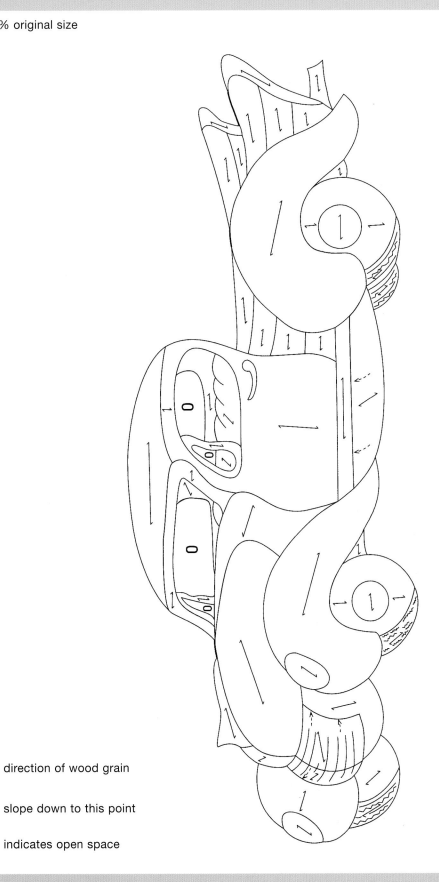

⟶   direction of wood grain

⇢   slope down to this point

0   indicates open space

Wolf

Wolf

I always imagine the wolf as a symbol of the wilderness — an example of wild freedom with its haunting howl echoing across the landscape. This is a great project for a cabin or family room. The detail gives it a realistic appearance. The eye in particular can give the wolf the expression you desire. I also used texturing to create the wolf's hair.

No. of pieces   47
Finished size   17 $\frac{1}{2}$ in x 13 in

Wood needed	Quantities
Black walnut	1 in x 2 in
Aspen	6 in x 14 in
Pau amarillo	6 in x 6 in
Poplar or sumac	3 in x 6 in
Dark WRC	4 in x 6 in
Medium dark WRC	6 in x 12 in
Medium WRC	6 in x 12 in
Light WRC	6 in x 12 in

Directions

1   Enlarge (p4) the pattern (p41) to the desired size.

2   Choose the wood you like (p5) or refer to the pattern suggestions. Begin with $\frac{3}{4}$ in thick material.

3   Transfer the pattern to the wood using any method explained on p4.

4   I made a few sets of eyes. I didn't glue the eyes down when I did the glue-up so I could take them out and see which ones looked best. I made a set look to right, left, straight ahead, and up a bit. A scroll saw is the best tool for cutting the pieces. Begin with a sharp blade and make sure it is square to the table. Refer to p7 for suggestions on blade size and style. Cut carefully on the line or just inside the line for more experienced scrollers. The eyes of the wolf are best made in a few steps. Cut the dowel from a board, cutting outside the traced line at a 5° angle. Mark the eye on a piece of light wood (photo 1), drill $\frac{5}{8}$ in hole (photo 2), insert yellow dowel (photos 3 & 4), drill $\frac{1}{4}$ in hole in the center of the yellow and insert $\frac{1}{4}$ in black dowel for the pupil. Cut the eye from the light board once the glue has dried (photo 5). Be particular with the placement of the pupils. This determines where the wolf is looking and gives the face expression and realism.

5   This project presents some fitting challenges. The jagged hair parts on the wolf's chest, below the chin, are a particular problem. Work on them separately until you have a good fit. Next get the face fitted and then fit it into the

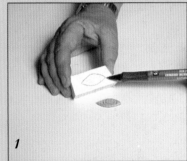

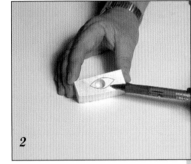

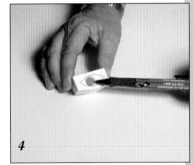

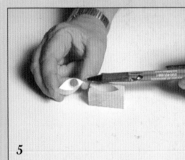

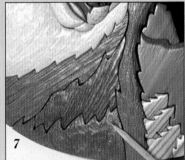

chest part. The background is fairly easy, except for the evergreens. When you have the pieces cut out, assemble them and check for fit. Refer to p9 for tips and suggestions on fitting this project.

6   Once you have the pieces fit to your liking raise and lower (p12) any pieces the pattern suggests. Raising and lowering will add perspective to the project. See photo 8.

7   Pay special attention to the wolf's nose. It should be raised and shaped to slope back to the face. As usual with an intarsia project it will look best seen from a certain angle. Do the shaping looking at it from the best angle. Assemble the pieces and mark on the reference lines (p13) to help with the shaping. Shaping is important for this project. The more time you spend the better the results. Aim for a realistic look. See p13 for tips on tools and techniques for shaping. At this point you can also texture (p15) the pieces to resemble hair. Use a wire wheel in a flex shaft. Wetting the surface of the wood will help achieve this look (photos 6 & 7, p 40).

8   Once the pieces are shaped, sand them to at least 220 grit.

9   Assemble the pieces on backing material, trace around them, remove the pieces, and cut out the backing board.

10   Glue the pieces onto the backing board (p16) with carpenter's glue. When the glue has dried, round the back edges of the backing board.

11   Apply the finish (p18) of your choice. Use at least 3 coats on the front and one on the back.

12   Attach a hanger (p18).

8

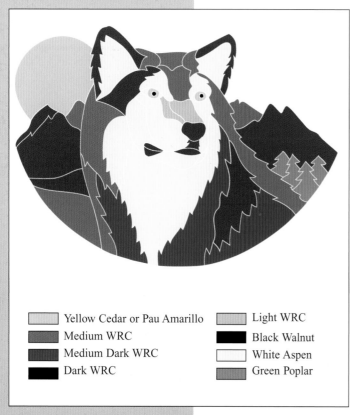

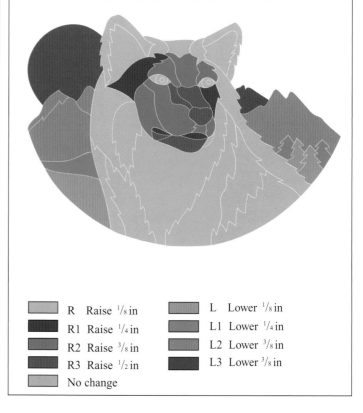

Yellow Cedar or Pau Amarillo	Light WRC		
Medium WRC	Black Walnut		
Medium Dark WRC	White Aspen		
Dark WRC	Green Poplar		

R Raise $^1/_8$ in	L Lower $^1/_8$ in
R1 Raise $^1/_4$ in	L1 Lower $^1/_4$ in
R2 Raise $^3/_8$ in	L2 Lower $^3/_8$ in
R3 Raise $^1/_2$ in	L3 Lower $^3/_8$ in
No change	

Pattern 50% original size

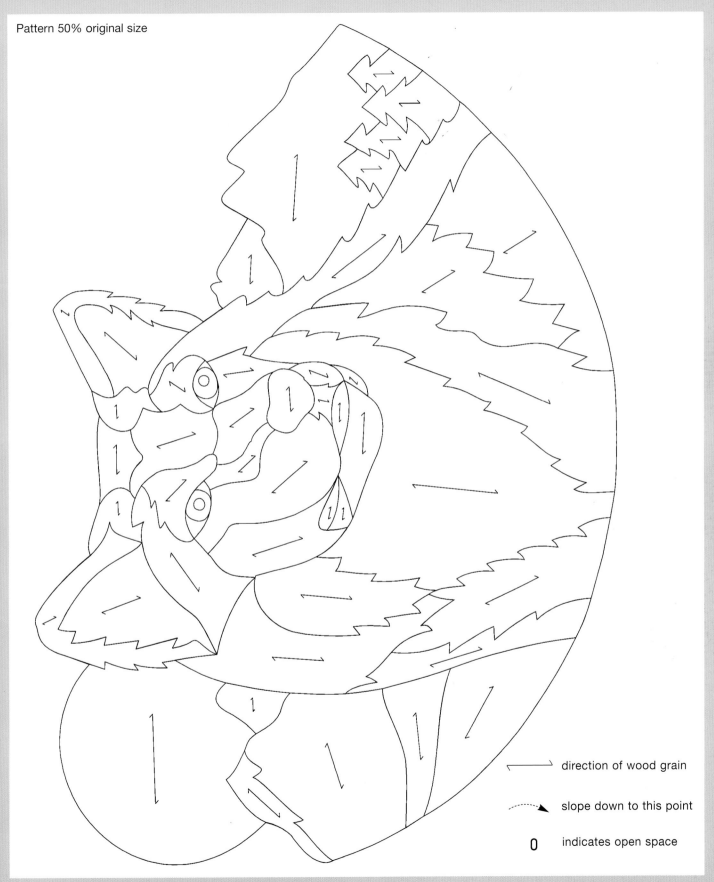

———————➤ direction of wood grain

· · · · · ·➤ slope down to this point

0 indicates open space

Ram's Head

Ram's Head

This is basically an ordinary intarsia project; however, shaping is important to achieve a realistic look for the curled horns. I tried some burnishing on the horns to make them look more natural. I also tried a new technique of shaping a number of pieces at one time. I used double-sided tape to attach the 3 neck pieces to a piece of scrap wood and sanded them together. I find this works very well.

No. of pieces   63
Finished size   15 in x 13 in

Wood needed	Quantities
Aspen	4 in x 4 in
Black walnut	2 in x 3 in
Dark WRC	4 in x 4 in
Medium dark WRC	4 in x 8 in
Medium WRC	4 in x 6 in
Light WRC	6 in x 12 in
Medium light WRC	4 in x 6 in

Directions

1 Enlarge (p4) the pattern (p45) to the desired size.
2 Choose the woods you want to use, referring to the pattern suggestions as a guide. Begin with ³/₄ in thick material. On the pattern I have suggested wood shades light and medium light. My suggestion is to find 2 light woods with some slight shade or grain difference, so they contrast each other.
3 Transfer the pattern to the wood (p4) with whichever method you prefer.
4 A scroll saw is the best tool to do the cutting. Begin with a new sharp blade. Refer to (p7) for blade choice. Make sure the blade is square to the table. Cut carefully on the line. If you are an experienced scroller try cutting just inside the line for a tighter fit.
5 I like to fit the face/neck area first and then get the large horn fitted into place and finally the small horn area. It can be difficult to get the horn parts to fit well so take your time. When you have the pieces cut out, assemble the project and check for fit. A light box is helpful to show gaps between the pieces. The width of a business card or credit card can be used as a guide. If the pieces don't fit fairly tight the gaps will detract from the finished look of the piece. Fitting can be tedious. Refer to the section on fitting (p9) for suggestions on how to obtain a tight fit.
6 Once the pieces fit to your liking, raise and lower any pieces the pattern suggests (p12). Shaping helps to achieve perspective. Pieces farthest away from you will be the thinnest and pieces closest will be the thickest (photo 3, p44).
7 Use a couple of shaping styles with this project. I tried to achieve a nice rounded transition shape with the face and neck. I wanted a rough style of shaping on the horns — two quite different shaping styles. Reassemble the project and mark on reference lines (p13) to assist with the shaping. Shape with whichever tool you prefer. See the section on shaping (p13). Try to achieve a

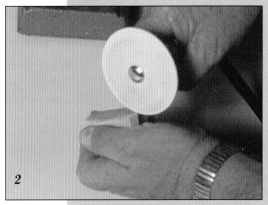

smooth transition from one level to the next. A good technique to achieve this is to attach a number of pieces to a piece of scrap wood and shape them together. Attach them with double sided tape or a glue gun (photo 1). The horns require special handling. You want the sections or rings to stand out from one another. Try some burnishing (p15) on the horns with a burnishing wheel to make them look more realistic (photo 2).

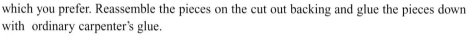

8   Once you have the shaping done, sand to at least 220 grit.

9   Assemble the pieces onto a backing board (p16), trace around them, remove the pieces, and cut out the back. You can make this project without a backing board. Refer to the section on backing (p16) for a description of this technique.

10   I glued this project in the same order as I fitted it. This is a project that could be made without a backing. You could experiment to find which you prefer. Reassemble the pieces on the cut out backing and glue the pieces down with ordinary carpenter's glue.

11   When the glue has dried, round off the back edge with a rounding over router bit or by sanding.

12   Apply the finish (p18) of your choice. Use at least 3 coats on the front and one on the back.

13   Attach a hanger (photo 4).

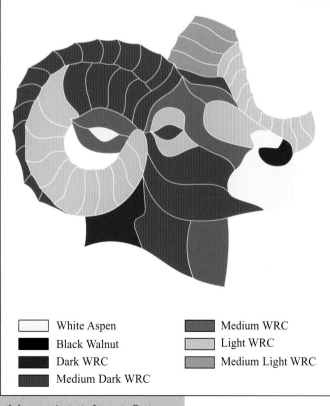

	White Aspen		Medium WRC
	Black Walnut		Light WRC
	Dark WRC		Medium Light WRC
	Medium Dark WRC		

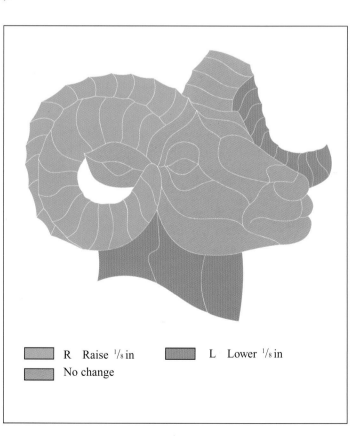

	R Raise ⅛ in		L Lower ⅛ in
	No change		

Pattern 50% original size

0

⟶ direction of wood grain

⟶ slope down to this point

0 indicates open space

Collie

Collie

I made this handsome Collie from natural wood colors to hang on my own wall. This is one of the most beloved dogs and people admire its intelligence and loyalty. You can make the intarsia Collie tri-color or the more traditional Lassie yellow and white. If you are looking for something special make a silver collie, using blue/gray pine.

No. of pieces   Traditional 36   Tri color 39
Finished size   18 in x 17 in

Tri Color

Wood needed	Quantities
Aspen	6 in x 18 in
Black walnut	6 in x 30 in
Medium dark WRC	4 in x 4 in
Medium WRC	4 in x 4 in
Light WRC	6 in x 16 in
Medium light WRC	4 in x 4 in

Traditional

Wood needed	Quantities
Aspen	6 in x 18 in
Black walnut	2 in x 2 in
Dark WRC	4 in x 8 in
Medium dark WRC	6 in x 10 in
Medium WRC	6 in x 16 in
Light WRC	6 in x 12 in

Directions

1 Enlarge the pattern (p49) to the desired size. A formula on (p4) will help you to enlarge it to the original size featured in the book.

2 Choose the wood. Because Collie colors are already defined, follow the pattern suggestions for a tri-colored Collie. If you choose different colors your Collie will not look the same. Begin with ³/₄ in material. I have marked the pattern to show wood choices for the two different styles. The pattern suggests medium light and light. To achieve this choose two light shades of WRC with different grain patterns or color variations to distinguish them.

3 Transfer (p4) the pattern to the wood with whichever method you prefer.

4 A scroll saw is the best tool for cutting the pieces. Begin with a sharp blade. Refer to p7 for blade choice. Make sure the blade is square to the table. Cut carefully on the line. If you are an experienced scroller try cutting just inside the line for a better fit off the saw.

5 There is no particular place to start the shaping, but with this project I fitted the face first and then worked down the body to the feet. I always like to get the hardest part fitted

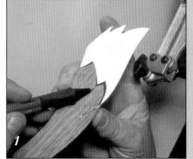
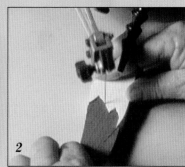

first. When you have the pieces cut out, assemble them and check for fit. Refer to the section on fitting (p9) for tips and suggestions on how tight the pieces should fit. Pieces that have zigzag edges can be difficult to fit. I usually use the saw blade for this. Fit the two pieces together the best you can and run a blade between them where they touch. This will define the edges for an easier fit (photo 1). Photo 2 shows blade in place where the pieces touch.

6 Once you have a good fit, raise and lower and pieces as the pattern directs to give perspective to the Collie (photo 3).

7 Shaping the Collie presents some of the same problems as the wolf. Pay special

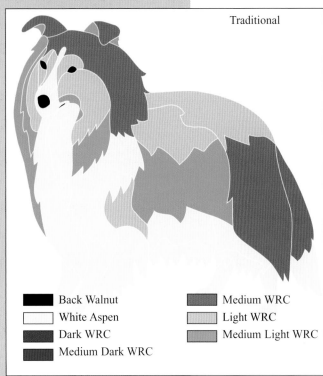

Traditional

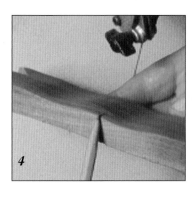

4

attention to the nose and face. Find the angle from which it looks best and check it from that angle as you go through the shaping process. Assemble the project and mark the reference lines (p13) to help with the shaping. Consult the section on shaping (p13) for tools and techniques for shaping. Try to shape the pieces to give a wavy look for the Collie's coat (photo 4)

8   Once the pieces are shaped sand them to at least 220 grit.

9   Assemble the pieces on a backing board (p16), trace around them, remove the pieces, and cut out the back. **Note**   This project can be made without a back.

10   I like to assemble the entire project onto the backing and then glue the pieces one at a time. If you glue the outside pieces first they will act as a frame to keep the other pieces in place. See step 11 before you glue up. Glue the pieces onto the backing with carpenter's glue and when dry, round the back edge.

11   Apply a finish of your choice (p18). If you want to keep the white wood as white as possible finish it separately with a water base clear finish. The other pieces can be finished with polyurethane. It's best to do this before you glue the pieces onto the backing.

12   Attach a hanger (p18).

■	Back Walnut	■	Medium WRC
□	White Aspen	■	Light WRC
■	Dark WRC	■	Medium Light WRC
■	Medium Dark WRC		

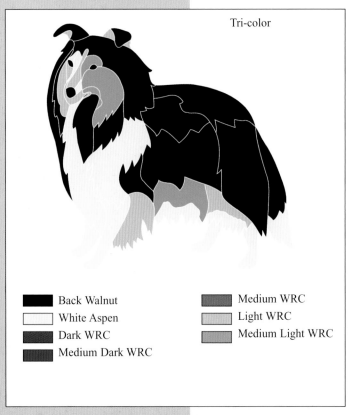

Tri-color

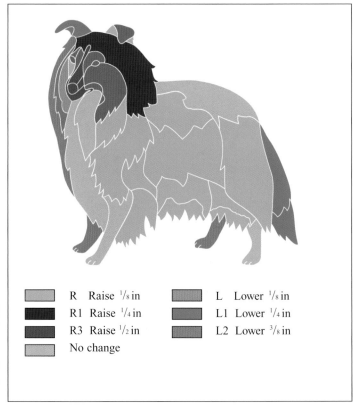

■	Back Walnut	■	Medium WRC
□	White Aspen	■	Light WRC
■	Dark WRC	■	Medium Light WRC
■	Medium Dark WRC		

■	R Raise $^1/_8$ in		■	L Lower $^1/_8$ in
■	R1 Raise $^1/_4$ in		■	L1 Lower $^1/_4$ in
■	R3 Raise $^1/_2$ in		■	L2 Lower $^3/_8$ in
■	No change			

Pattern 40% original size

→ direction of wood grain

⇢ slope down to this point

0 indicates open space

Candle Holder

Candle Holder

I have made this simple yet delightful craft project for years to give as gifts for Christmas. The candle holder with its colorful candle conveys warm feelings from your house to a friend. The colored woods make this project stand out.

No. of pieces	22
Finished size	10 ½ in x 8 ½ in

Wood needed	Quantities
Pau amarillo	4 in x 10 in
Poplar, or sumac	4 in x 8 in
Bloodwood, or padauk	2 in x 2 in
Yellow cedar, or pine	2 in x 4 in
Aspen, or holly, or spruce	2 in x 4 in

Directions

1 Enlarge (p4) the pattern (p52) to the desired size. This project looks best at the actual size in the book. See p4 for sizing information.

2 Choose woods that you like or refer to the pattern suggestions. Yc indicates a pale yellow and I used yellow cedar (photo 1) although ponderosa pine also comes in a pale yellow color and this is also suitable. The easiest to find source of green is poplar (photo 2), which often has boards with green streaks, or verawood. You can make the berries red using bloodwood or padauk (photo 2). Try to pick out the most distinct color. Begin with ¾ in material.

3 Transfer (p4) the pattern to the wood using the method of your choice.

4 The red berries around the leaves can present a fitting problem. It might be easier if you extend the leaves a bit, glue the project up, and then very carefully drill or use padauk or bloodwood dowels. I used a ⅜ in plug cutter to make small dowels from exotic woods. A scroll saw is the best tool for cutting out the pieces. Refer to p7 for blade choice, making sure the blade used is square to the table. Cut carefully on the line or just inside the line if you are an experienced scroller.

5 When the pieces are cut out, assemble them and check for fit. Refer to p9 for tips and suggestions on fitting.

6 Raise and lower any pieces the pattern suggests. This project has a lot of raised and lowered pieces, which add to the detail and make the project more interesting (photo 3).

7 Assemble the project and add reference lines (p13) to help with the shaping. Shape the pieces carefully to give it more perspective.

8 Once the pieces are shaped sand to at least 220 grit.

9 Assemble the pieces on the backing material (p16), trace around them, remove the pieces, and cut out the back.

10 Glue the pieces onto the backing with carpenter's glue.

11 Apply the finish (p18) of your choice. Use at least 3 coats on the front and one on the back.

12 Attach a hanger (p18).

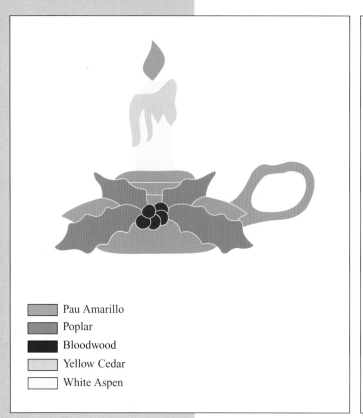

	Pau Amarillo
	Poplar
	Bloodwood
	Yellow Cedar
	White Aspen

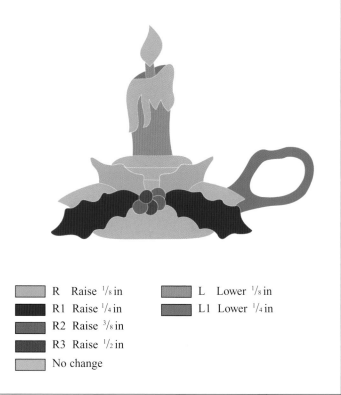

	R Raise $^1/_8$ in			L Lower $^1/_8$ in
	R1 Raise $^1/_4$ in			L1 Lower $^1/_4$ in
	R2 Raise $^3/_8$ in			
	R3 Raise $^1/_2$ in			
	No change			

Pattern 50% original size

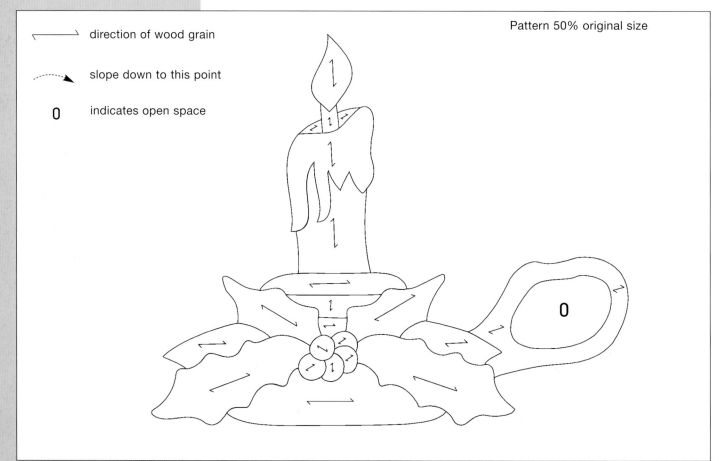

→ direction of wood grain

⇢ slope down to this point

0 indicates open space

Drummer Boy

Drummer Boy

This is a fun project that is easy to make. Hardwoods look the best here. Western red cedar, the traditional wood for intarsia, also works well, but I prefer hardwoods. To me, they make a project look richer and give it a more artistic look. This is an excellent project for Christmas, for the home or for gifts.

No. of pieces   45
Finished size   14 in x 10 in

Wood needed	Quantities
Mahogany	6 in x 10 in
Aspen	3 in x 6 in
Yellow cedar	3 in x 4 in
Cherry	4 in x 6 in
Pine	1 in x 2 in
Alder	3 in x 4 in
Purpleheart	2 in x 4 in
Pau amarillo	3 in x 2 in
Black walnut	2 in x 4 in

Directions

1   Enlarge (p4) the pattern (p56) to the size you wish.
2   Choose the woods you prefer (p4) or follow the suggestions on the pattern. Begin with ³/₄ in material.
3   Transfer the pattern using any of the methods described on p4.
4   Use a scroll saw for cutting out the pieces. Make sure the blade is sharp and square to the table. A #7 P/S style blade is a good blade to use for intarsia.
5   The area of the drum can be hard to fit so start there. Small pieces are often the hardest to fit. The smallest overcut on any piece can cause a problem. The rest of the project is fairly easy. When you have all the pieces cut out assemble them and check the fit. A reasonable fit is important but the pieces don't have to fit airtight. I like to use a credit card or business card as fit gauges. The amount of space to slide in a credit card is the maximum space acceptable, but try for a space the width of a business card.
6   When you have the pieces fit to your liking, raise and lower any pieces the pattern suggests (p14). See photo 1 for different wood thicknesses.
7   Give the drummer boy pieces a nice rounded look. Shape the pieces so they flow from one to another. The drum also should have a rounded look. Remember, you are adding perspective with the shaping as well as the raising and lowering. Assemble the pieces and draw reference lines (p13) to help with the shaping. The different levels add perspective to the piece and the shaping will give it realism. The more shaping you do the better the project will look. Try to achieve a smooth transition from one level to the next.
8   Once the pieces are shaped sand them to 220 grit. Cut out the buttons for the drum from

1

dark wood and set into yellow drum wood (photo 2). Use a burning tool to make the lines on the drum (photo3). I cut the mouth lines on the scroll saw. The fingers are from one piece of wood with the finger separations carved in. The button on the cuff in ¼ in walnut dowel.

9   Reassemble the pieces onto the backing board (p16), trace around them, then remove the pieces and cut out the back.

10   Start with the small pieces of the drum. Get them glued and in place, then work your way around the piece. It's best to not get any glue on the sides of pieces that might squeeze to the surface and cause finish problems. After the glue dries it will be difficult to see until you apply a finish and then there will be a white spot or blotch. If you try to sand them out it will get worse. The heat from the abrasive will melt the glue and spread it over a greater area as well as deeper into the wood. You can scrape the glue out with a cabinet scraper or chisel, but sometimes it's still visible. Assemble the pieces on the cut out back and start the glue-up. Use an ordinary carpenter's glue.

11   When the glue has dried round over the back.

12   Apply the finish of your choice (p18).

13   Attach a hanger (p18).

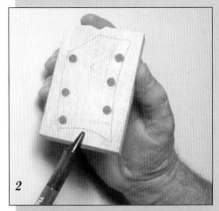

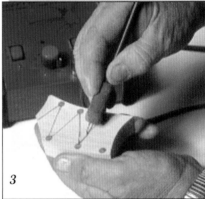

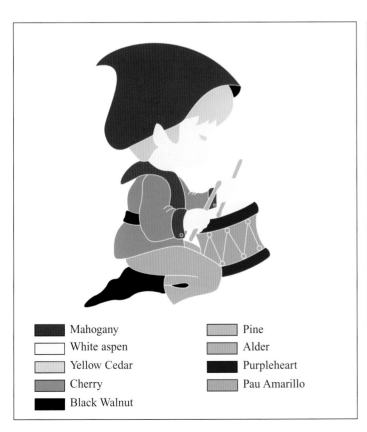

	Mahogany		Pine
	White aspen		Alder
	Yellow Cedar		Purpleheart
	Cherry		Pau Amarillo
	Black Walnut		

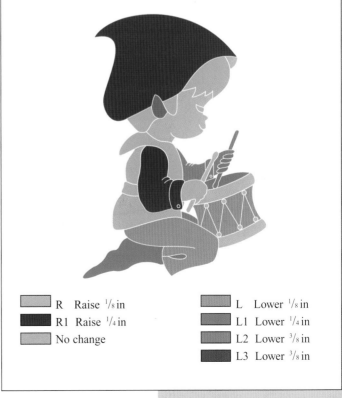

R	Raise ¹/₈ in		L	Lower ¹/₈ in
R1	Raise ¹/₄ in		L1	Lower ¹/₄ in
	No change		L2	Lower ³/₈ in
			L3	Lower ³/₈ in

Pattern 55% original size

direction of wood grain

slope down to this point

0   indicates open space
small open spaces are
optional

Astral Mirror

Astral Mirror

I designed this project so the mirror can be removed for cleaning. The project is quite straightforward and fairly easy to make. Wood choice can have an effect on the outcome. The project has great appeal to all those interested in astrology and is quite a conversation piece.

No. of pieces   25
Finished size   17 in diameter

Wood needed	Quantities
Pau amarillo	6 in x 16 in
Spalted blue spruce or pine	6 in x 12 in
Light WRC	2 in x 4 in
Gray poplar or mahogany	3 in x 6 in
Black walnut	2 in x 2 in
Dark WRC	2 in x 4 in
Medium WRC	2 in x 2 in
Green poplar	3 in x 8 in

Directions

1   Enlarge (p4) the pattern (p60) to the size desired. To enlarge to the original size see p4 for suggestions on how to do this.
2   Choose the wood (p5) for the project paying special attention to wood shades and grain direction. Choice of woods and grains is a very artistic step which will affect how your project turns out. Use the pattern suggestions as a guide but feel free to use your own imagination. Begin with ³/₄ in thick material.
3   Transfer (p4) the pattern to the wood with whichever method you prefer.
4   Cut out the pieces with a scroll saw. Make sure the table is square with the blade. Begin with a #7 double tooth or skip tooth blade. I tried a #3 hook tooth blade and found that it cuts as fast as a skip tooth but leaves a smaller kerf and allows a slightly better fit. If you use the template pattern method try cutting just inside the line for a better fit.
5   This project is fairly easy to fit. The fish is the hardest part and I began with it, then proceeded to the dolphin. The wave pieces can also present some challenge. When you have all the pieces cut out assemble the project and check for fit. See p14 for hints on fitting. As long as the gaps are no bigger than a credit card thickness you are within tolerances.

6   Raise and lower any pieces the pattern suggests (p12). This will give perspective (photo 1).
7   Reassemble the project and mark on reference lines (p13). These lines will help with the shaping.
8   Shape the pieces to achieve the look of a relief carving making a smooth transition from one level to the next. The more shaping you do the better the project will look. Round the moon face as much as possible. The sky and water parts are fairly flat. Round fish, dolphin, and tree. Make sure there are no saw marks or burn marks in the cut out parts. Pay special attention to the edge of the pieces to make sure they are free of saw cuts. If not they will be reflected in the mirror and be more visible.

1

9 Sand all the pieces to 220 grit. Sanding to a higher grit makes more dust; however it's a personal choice if you want to go to 600 grit. If you are using a paste type finish or want to use a water base finish on some white parts now is the time to do it.

10 I glued the moon first. You may have to clamp it down in order for it to lie flat. After the glue has dried 15 to 20 minues, carry on with the gluing. Glue up around the outside and finish off with the inside pieces. Since this project has a mirror, it can act as a backing, and you can make the project without the usual backing (p16). This project is delicate so be careful with it. The drum sander works well for sanding the back of this project. I chose to glue it to a thin $^1/_8$ in backing and painted the edges black (photo 2). I attached the mirror with 4 small #4 wood screws $^1/_2$ in long. Rubber washers will help to prevent the glass from breaking as you tighten the screws, or use some small pieces of vinyl with a hole (photo 3). This allows the mirror to be removed for cleaning

11 Make a template of the mirror from cardboard and make holes for the screws, making sure they line up with solid wood (photo 4). Make sure you mark on the template which side is the mirror. Take the mirror to a glass shop and have the holes drilled. I had mine drilled $^3/_{16}$ in. Make a cut out in the mirror for the hanger.

12 Apply your choice of finish (p18) to the project. Use 3 coats on the front and one on the back and sand between coats. Attach the mirror. Glue pieces onto the mirror with a glue that bonds wood to glass. I used *WeldBond*.

13 Attach the hanger (photo 5).

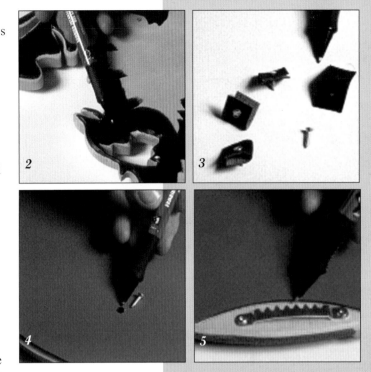

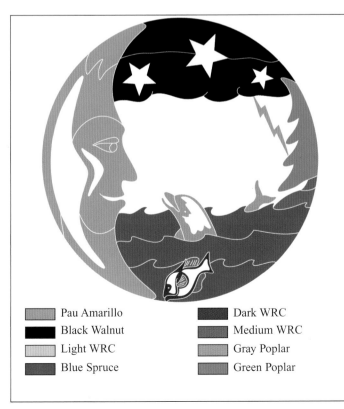

Pau Amarillo		Dark WRC	
Black Walnut		Medium WRC	
Light WRC		Gray Poplar	
Blue Spruce		Green Poplar	

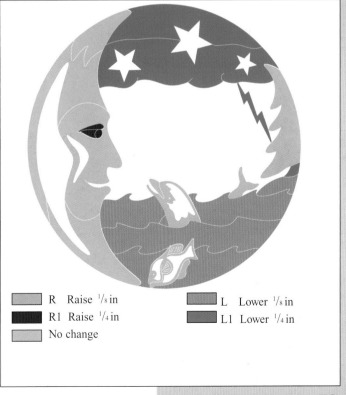

R Raise $^1/_8$ in		L Lower $^1/_8$ in	
R1 Raise $^1/_4$ in		L1 Lower $^1/_4$ in	
No change			

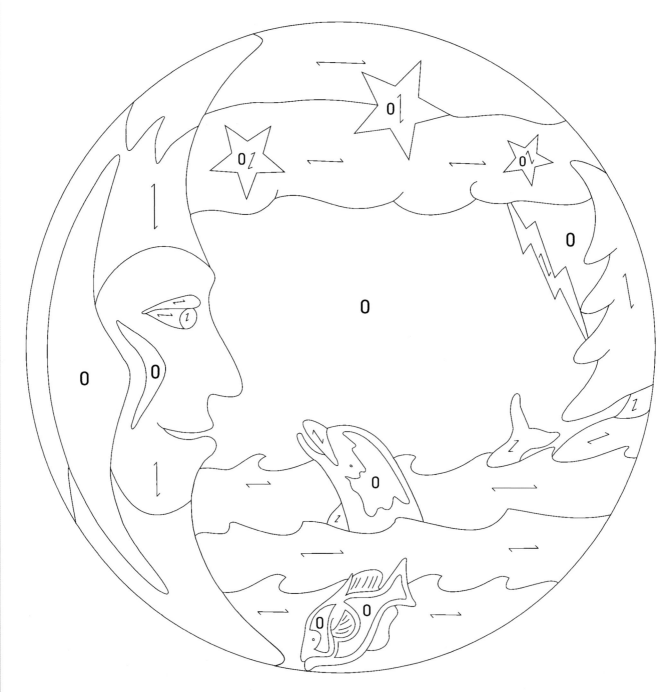

direction of wood grain

slope down to this point

0   indicates open space

Toucan

Toucan

This jungle bird adds richness to any room. The project is interesting to make and you can create a very artistic effect with some fine shaping. I chose traditional intarsia wood but you can choose more brilliant woods or even paint the project. I used a burnishing tool to burn veins on leaves. This is a very popular gift.

No. of pieces   38
Finished size   18 ½ in x 15 in

Wood needed	Quantities
Black walnut	6 in x 16 in
Aspen	4 in x 6 in
Bloodwood or padauk	1 in x 1 in
Medium WRC	2 in x 8 in
Pau amarillo	3 in x 8 in
Poplar or sumac or verawood	4 in x 24 in

Directions

1   Enlarge (p4) the pattern (p64) size desired.
2   Choose the woods (p5) you like or follow the colors suggested in the pattern. Begin with ¾ in material.
3   Transfer the pattern to the wood with one of the techniques on p4.
4   Cut out the pieces with a scroll saw. Make sure the blade is square to the table. Use a blade of your choice but a #7 P/S or DT/R works well. Cut carefully to save yourself a lot of fitting problems. Try cutting just inside the line for a better fit. **Note**   The toucan's eye can be a bit tricky to make. I like to start by cutting out the larger yellow part. Then cut out the center part and trace this opening onto some white wood. Cut the white part out cutting just outside the line. Then cut the center part of the white piece out. Make sure the white part fits into the yellow part. Trace the center part of the white piece onto some black wood. Cut the black part out cutting just outside the line. Now fit the black part into the white part. At this point you can glue it up and sand the piece as one. This will give it a flat look. Another way is to raise the black part ⅛ in and the white part about 1/16 in. Then shape the black part down to the white and the white part down to the yellow, giving the eye a more rounded look. A little extra time spent on the eyes of a project will bring it to life.
5   With this project I fitted the wing parts together, then fitted them into the body, and then the rest of the bird. The hardest part is where the legs and tree limb attach to the body. Do it next. The leaves fit fairly easily. Assemble the bird and check the fit. If the space between pieces is within a saw kerf or width of a business card that is acceptable. If these gaps are larger they require more tedious fitting. See the section on fitting (p9) for tips .
6   Once the pieces are fitted to your liking, raise and lower (p12) any pieces the pattern suggests. This gives perspective (photo 1).
7   Try to give the bird's body a rounded look. Round the wing, which is the center and highest part of the body. Slope from there down to the outside of the body. The beak also

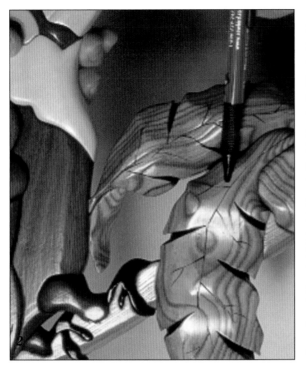

requires a lot of shaping to give it a rounded look. I tried to give the leaves a wavy look, making them look more realistic. Reassemble the project and mark reference lines (p13) to help with the shaping. This is a critical step for this project. A careful shaping will bring the project to life. The more you shape this bird the better it will look. Use a burning tool to make vein lines in leaves (photo 2).

8   Once the shaping is done sand the pieces to 220 grit.

9   Assemble the project on a backing board (p16), trace around pieces, remove the pieces, and cut out the backing. This isn't a good project to construct with no backing.

10   Reassemble the pieces on the backing and start the glue-up with ordinary carpenter's glue. Photo 1 shows the thicknesses of various levels.

11   When the glue has dried round the back edges.

12   Apply the finish (p18) of your choice. Use 3 coats on front and one on the back.

13   Attach a hanger (p18).

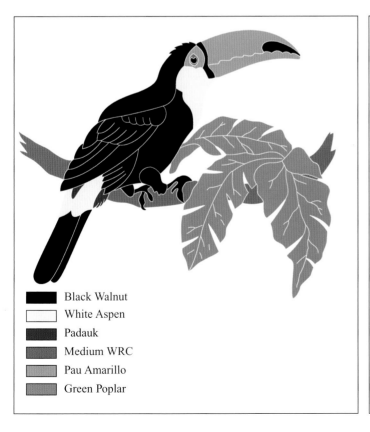

- ■ Black Walnut
- □ White Aspen
- ■ Padauk
- ▨ Medium WRC
- ▨ Pau Amarillo
- ▨ Green Poplar

▨	R Raise ¹/₈ in		▨	L Lower ¹/₈ in
■	R1 Raise ¹/₄ in		▨	L1 Lower ¹/₄ in
▨	R2 Raise ³/₈ in		▨	L2 Lower ³/₈ in
▨	No change			

Pattern 40% original size

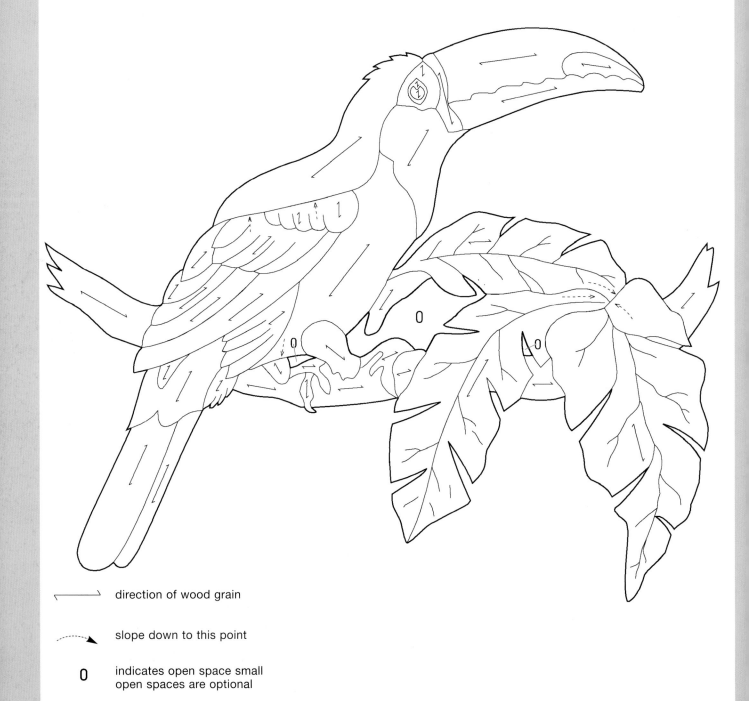

→ direction of wood grain

⇢ slope down to this point

0 indicates open space small
   open spaces are optional

Bear on the Moon

Bear on the Moon

A teddy bear swinging on the moon is a fun project for a child's room. The perky bear is everyone's favorite. Not too difficult, it has a small finishing surprise.

No. of pieces   55
Finished size   16 in x 17 in

Wood needed	Quantities
Aspen or holly or spruce	6 in x 12 in
Black walnut	2 in x 2 in
Pau amarillo	6 in x 24 in
Dark WRC	6 in x 8 in
Bloodwood or padauk	4 in x 8 in
Light WRC	4 in x 6 in
Medium WRC	2 in x 4 in
Yellow cedar or pine	4 in x 12 in

Directions

1 Enlarge (p4) the pattern (p68) to the original size. See the formula on p4 to show you how to enlarge the pattern to the same size as the original.

2 Choose the woods you prefer or refer to the pattern suggestions. For the yellow color you can use yellow cedar or pine. Yellow cedar is a pale yellow color, and you can often find pine with a pale yellow shade as well.

3 Transfer the pattern to the wood using whichever method you prefer (p4).

4 A scroll saw is better than a band saw for cutting. Begin with a sharp blade (see blade choice on p8). Make sure the blade is square to the table. Cut carefully on the line or just inside the line for a little better fit.

5 The bear itself is the hardest part to fit and a great place to start the fitting. Fit the small inside pieces and work from there. The larger parts are not too hard to fit. When all the pieces are cut out, assemble the project and check the fit. A light box can be helpful to locate the gaps. However, the pieces don't have to fit airtight. Small gaps such as a saw kerf or the width of a credit card are acceptable. But make sure that any gaps don't detract from the look of the piece. Fitting can be tedious. See p9 for suggestions on how to get the best fitting results.

1

6 Once the project is fitted raise and lower (p12) any pieces suggested in the pattern. Raising and lowering will give your work perspective. Pieces farthest away from you will be thinner and the closest pieces the thickest (photo 1).

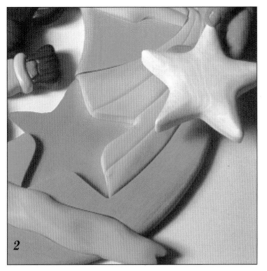

2

7 The bear should be shaped in a round traditional style. The moon parts are only slightly rounded on the edges. The clouds can have more shaping. Reassemble the project and mark the reference lines to help with the shaping. Try to achieve a smooth transition from one level to the next. Use the abrasive tools you prefer (p13) for shaping.

8 Once the pieces are shaped sand them to at least 220 grit. I don't go past 220 grit; mainly to reduce the amount of dust that sanding to a higher grit would create.

9 Assemble the project on the backing board, trace

3

around it, remove the pieces, and cut out the back. Although you can glue a project together without a backing, this technique is not recommended for this project.

10 Reassemble the pieces on the cut out back. Use carpenter's glue to glue all the pieces except the star, which needs to be removable (photo 2).

11 When the glue has dried round the back edge (photo 3).

12 Apply a finish (p18) of your choice to all the project except the star. Use a water base clear high gloss on the star to keep it as white as possible. Glue in place only when the project has been finished. Sand between coats.

13 Attach a hanger (p18).

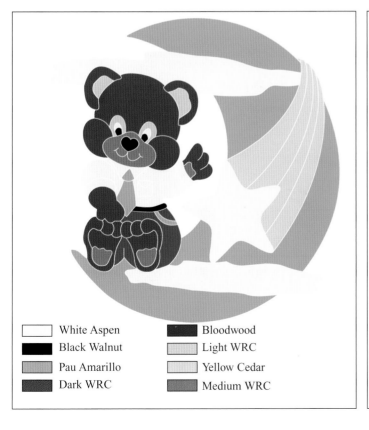

	White Aspen		Bloodwood
	Black Walnut		Light WRC
	Pau Amarillo		Yellow Cedar
	Dark WRC		Medium WRC

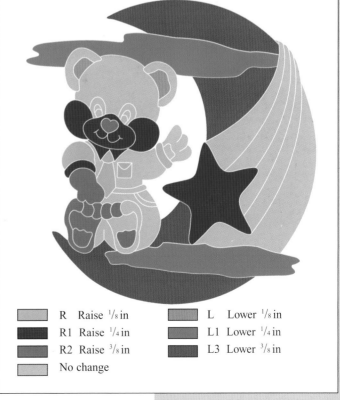

	R	Raise $^1/_8$ in		L	Lower $^1/_8$ in
	R1	Raise $^1/_4$ in		L1	Lower $^1/_4$ in
	R2	Raise $^3/_8$ in		L3	Lower $^3/_8$ in
		No change			

Pattern 40% original size

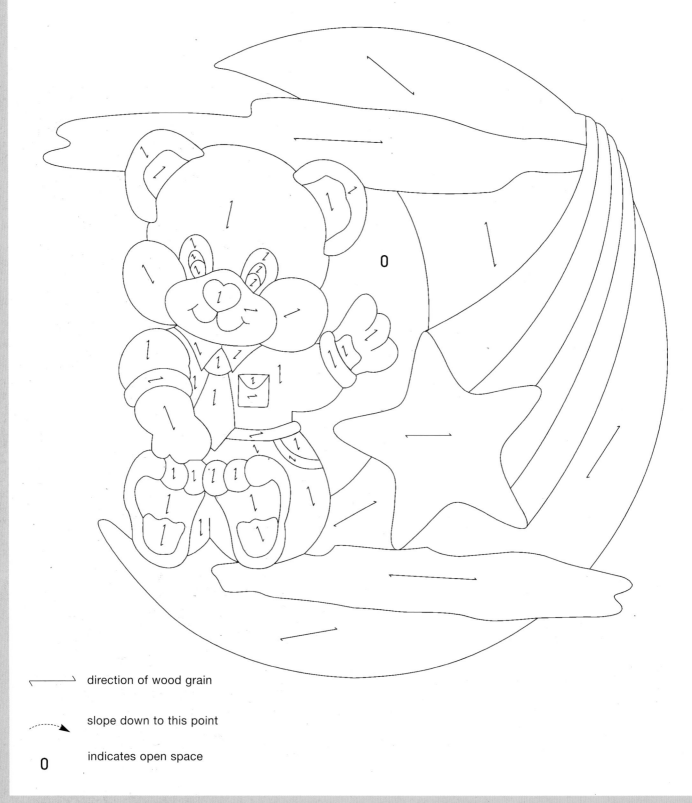

——————→ direction of wood grain

- - - → slope down to this point

0 indicates open space

Artistic Intarsia Projects

Haida Loon

Haida Loon

The art of the West Coast natives is one of my favorite art forms. Haida, Salish, Nootka, Kwagiutl, Tlingit, and Tsimshian live along the coast from Washington to the Yukon and the rich symbolism of the forms they create has always inspired me. Their work is mainly carved out of western red cedar and color is added, usually only black and red. This project is my interpretation of one of their traditional designs. With intarsia we are able to add different shades of cedar in black, red, and white colors.

No. of pieces   53
Finished size   16 in x 8 ¹/₂ in

Wood needed	Quantities
Aspen	4 in x 8 in
Bloodwood	3 in x 6 in
Dark WRC	6 in x 18 in
Medium light WRC	3 in x 6 in
Medium WRC	3 in x 6 in
Light WRC	1 in x 2 in

Directions

1   Enlarge the pattern (p72) to the original size (p4).
2   Choose the woods you want to use. I suggest more traditional colors and shades of woods for this project. Begin with ³/₄ in material. For suggested LT and MLT, use two light shades of western red cedar that have different grain patterns and shades.
3   Transfer the pattern to the wood with whichever technique you prefer (p4).
4   Begin cutting the pieces but do not cut the pieces that are inside other pieces at this time. Take your time and cut on the line. Careful cutting will improve the fit and save a lot of time with fitting. See p8 for suggestions on blades and sizes. Make sure your blade is square to the table.
5   Fit first all the pieces with other pieces fit inside them. Once these were fitted I could fit them to surrounding pieces and bring the project together. It is a fairly hard project to fit

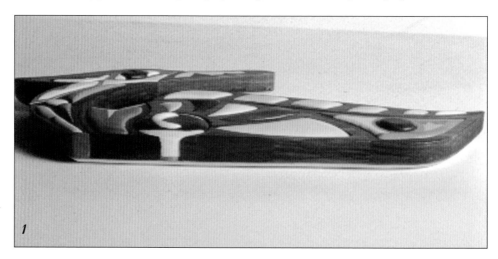

1

nicely, so take your time. Assemble the cut-out pieces and check for fit. The pieces should fit well but need not be airtight (p9). This project has a number of inside fitting pieces that are cut from the outside pieces which were cut first (photo2) Cut outside piece first, then trace inside piece onto selected wood. Be sure to cut outside the line (photo 3). The blade is inserted inside the line to finally fit the piece (photo 4). Photo 5 shows the finished fit.

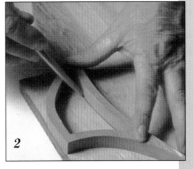

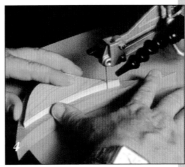
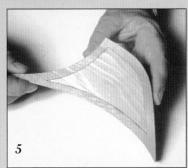
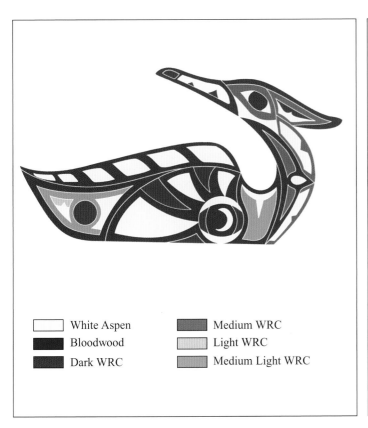

6   Once the pieces fit well, raise and lower pieces as the pattern suggests to give perspective (photo 1).

7   Reassemble the project and mark reference lines which will help with the shaping.

8   Now sand all the pieces to at least 220 grit.

9   This project is fine without a backing but it's a matter of personal choice. For a project with backing, assemble the project onto the backing material, trace around it, and remove the pieces. Cut out.

10   I did the glue-up in a similar order as I did the fitting. Glue the pieces with inside pieces first and then glue around the outside and work in. Reassemble the pieces on the cut out back and start to glue with ordinary carpenter's glue.

11   When the glue has dried, round the back edge.

12   Apply the finish (p18) of your choice. Use three coats on the front and one on the back. Sand between coats.

13   Attach a hanger (p18).

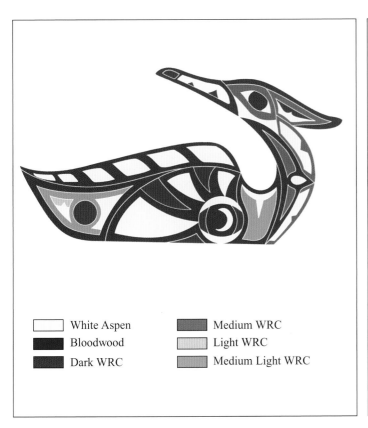
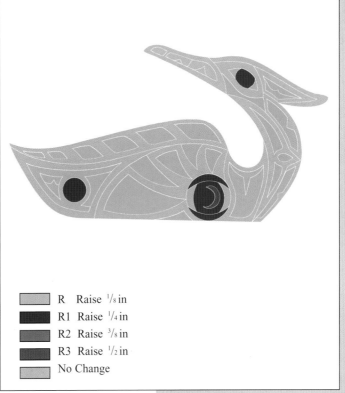

	White Aspen		Medium WRC
	Bloodwood		Light WRC
	Dark WRC		Medium Light WRC

	R	Raise 1/8 in
	R1	Raise 1/4 in
	R2	Raise 3/8 in
	R3	Raise 1/2 in
		No Change

Pattern 50% original size

→ direction of wood grain

⤳ slope down to this point

0 indicates open space

Draft Horse

Draft Horse

Everyone loves a horse. Here we have a faithful old work horse harnessed up for a day's work. This project is fairly difficult. It involves a number of small pieces that require extra careful cutting so everything will fit. Detail is added by wood burning. All harness parts and collar parts are black walnut, the harness reins and snaps are pau amarillo.

No. of pieces   34
Finished size   17 in x 17 in

Wood needed	Quantities
Aspen	3 in x 10 in
Black walnut	8 in x 48 in
Pau amarillo	4 in x 8 in
Medium light WRC	6 in x 12 in
Medium dark WRC	6 in x 10 in
Light WRC	7 in x 30 in
Dark WRC	1 in x 4 in
Medium WRC	6 in x 10 in

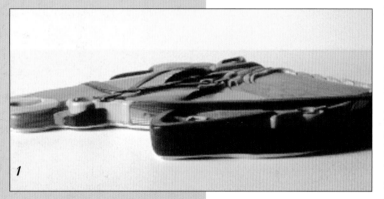

1

Directions

1 Enlarge the pattern (p76) to the original size (p4).
2 Choose the woods you want to use, referring to the pattern suggestions as a guide. The harness should be black but the horse can be whatever color you like. I used some hardwoods on this project. They make the project look richer and more life-like. Begin with ³/₄ in thick material. Hardwoods are also harder to cut. I have found that a hook tooth style blade will cut hardwoods better. I routinely cut ³/₄ in walnut and oak with a #3 hook tooth blade. It's the only blade that I have found that will cut bloodwood and purpleheart without burning. A blade lubricant will also help reduce friction, so blades will cut faster. Change blade more often when cutting hardwoods. A dull blade will cause you to push harder and you will end up with a poor quality cut that will cause fitting problems.
3 Transfer the pattern to the wood using any of the methods on p4.
4 Cut out the pieces carefully. See p8 for suggestions about blades for cutting. Cut on the line or just inside the line for a better fit.
5 When all the pieces are cut out assemble and check for fit. Fitting this project is difficult and requires patience. The harness lines divide the project. I started with the horse's face, then forehead, then mane and neck above the reins, and finally the collar and parts below the reins. The pieces don't have to fit airtight but should be no more than a saw kerf apart.
6 Once the pieces are fitted to your liking, raise and lower (p12) the pieces suggested in the pattern. Raising and lowering gives the project perspective (photo 1). The parts of the project farthest away from you will be the thinnest. Pieces closest to you will be the thickest.
7 This project demands a lot of attention to the shaping to bring it to life. Some areas require more shaping than others. The reins and harness parts should be lightly shaped. You

want a flat look for them. The horse collar should be rounded as well as the harness rings. The horse itself should be well rounded. You can texture the mane with a wire wheel. Make the eye well rounded, add a small $1/8$ in dowel to give a sparkle to the eye. Reassemble and mark the reference lines (p13). Try to achieve a smooth transition from one level to the next. You are trying to achieve the look of relief carving.

8   Once you have the project shaped, sand all the pieces to 220 grit. Now it's time for a little wood burning to add detail and make the harness look more realistic. Burn stitching lines on the harness (photo2).

9   Assemble the project onto a backing board, trace around it, remove the pieces, and cut out the back. You can also make this project without a backing board (p16).

10   Because of it's size this project can be a challenge to glue up. Make sure you have a good fit on the backing board before you start. I like to glue around the outside to form a frame and work inward checking the fit. It can take most of a afternoon to get a good glue-up with this project. Reassemble the pieces on the cut out backing and glue the pieces down with carpenter's glue.

11   When the glue has dried, round off the back edge with a rounding over router bit or by sanding.

12   Apply the finish (p18) of your choice. Put three coats on the front and one on the back. Sand between coats.

13   Attach a hanger (p18).

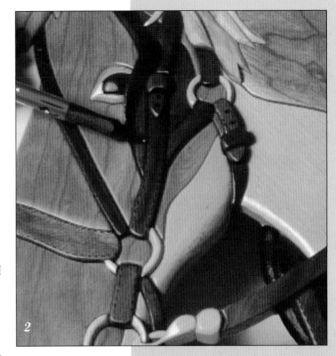

2

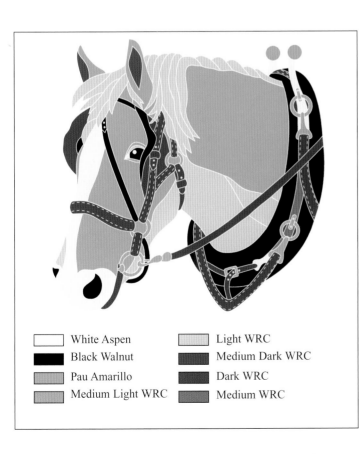

☐	White Aspen	☐	Light WRC
■	Black Walnut	☐	Medium Dark WRC
☐	Pau Amarillo	☐	Dark WRC
☐	Medium Light WRC	☐	Medium WRC

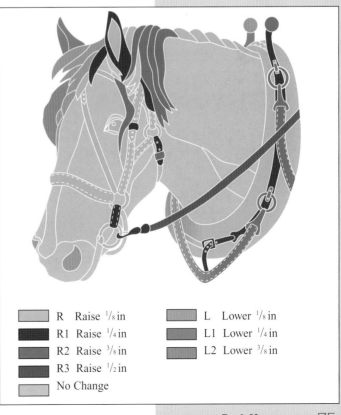

☐	R Raise $1/8$ in	☐	L Lower $1/8$ in
■	R1 Raise $1/4$ in	☐	L1 Lower $1/4$ in
☐	R2 Raise $3/8$ in	☐	L2 Lower $3/8$ in
☐	R3 Raise $1/2$ in		
☐	No Change		

Pattern 40% original size

—————➤ direction of wood grain

········➤ slope down to this point

0   indicates open space

Clam Clock

Clam Clock

I designed this project to demonstrate Gord Armstrong's (p10) Mirror Imaging Tool (MIT). This simple-to-use system allows you to make perfectly fitting intarsia and inlay projects. This is my opportunity to show everyone how it works using this clock project. The clock is quite unusual and can be used in any room.

No. of pieces   24
Finished size $14 \frac{1}{2}$ in x $11 \frac{1}{2}$ in

Wood needed	Quantities
Light WRC	6 in x 36 in
Dark WRC	6 in x 24 in

Directions

1   Enlarge the pattern (p81) to desired size.
2   Glue Arborite (plastic laminate) to $\frac{1}{4}$ in baltic birch plywood (Photo 1) that is large enough for the project. **Note** Arborite (plastic laminate) is used for counter tops. It is less than $\frac{1}{16}$ in thick and very hard. The template is made from this material for the bearing to ride on.

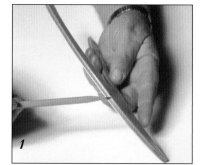

3   Transfer (p4) the pattern to the template material. If you use light colored Arborite you can trace the pattern onto it with graphite paper or you can attach the pattern with a spray adhesive.
4   Cut out the template using a small blade (2/0 double tooth for new scrollers or a hook tooth for more experienced scrollers). Cut the template carefully. It is the first step toward a good final product. See the section on accurate cutting for tips on cutting on line (p6).
5   Trace the template onto the wood of choice, using a sharp pencil held at a 45° angle (photo 2).
6   Cut around each piece approximately $\frac{1}{16}$ in outside the line (photo 3), as close as you can without touching the

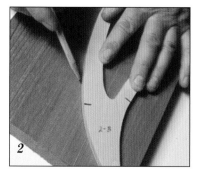

line. Any extra material will be milled off with the MIT. Make sure the blade is square to the table (p7) and use a blade of choice (p8) for the material (photo 4).

7   Attach the correct template piece to the corresponding cutout piece. Double-sided tape will hold the pieces securely. Cover all the surface on small pieces (photo 5).

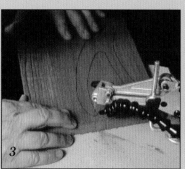

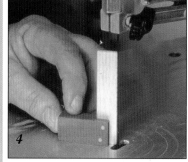

8   Begin the milling process with the largest MIT the shape will allow. The only limiting factor of this tool is the size of the inside curves of projects. In these difficult cases you must resort back to traditional methods of cutting accurately. However, the MIT system handles almost all situations and allows anyone to make perfect intarsia and inlay fits. **Note**   The 50 grit MIT (photo 6) is adequate for intarsia and most other applications. There are 80 and 150 grit MIT's available for different materials and even tighter fits. You can actually fit one piece inside another piece with a fit so tight that it will stay in place by friction alone and does not have to be glued. Photo 7 shows three MITs.

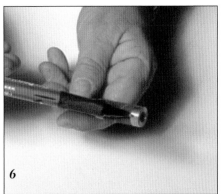

9   Chuck the MIT into your drill press. Make sure the bearing is riding on the arborite (photo 8). Check to make sure the MIT is square to the table. Photo 9 shows cleaning the MIT Drum, with a piece of rubber arborite cleaner.

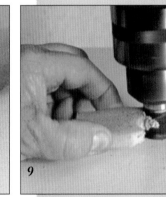

10   Use light pressure as you begin milling and allow the tool to do the work. It's better to make multiple passes with the MIT, keeping the abrasive clean with a piece of belt cleaner (photo 9). **Note**   The MIT will mill any wood, soft or hard. Hardwood may require an extra pass. This system creates sawdust, but it is easily handled with a dust collector mounted on the drill press (photo 10). Photo 11 shows dust collector box.

11   Mill all the pieces. Remove the template pieces from the project pieces with a utility knife. Slip the blade between the template and the piece. Apply a twisting pressure and gently pry them apart, being careful with very small pieces. Assemble for fit. With this method all the pieces fit tight the first time. **Note**   Without using the MIT system, this project is difficult to fit. You will see that all the points come tightly together using this system.

12   Proceed as in a normal intarsia or inlay project. Shape and sand as usual.

Note   If you do not use the MIT, the project can be made the same way as any regular intarsia project. The raising and lowering procedure gives the clam shell its character (photo 12).

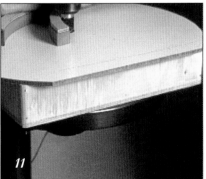

13   To install the clock mechanism drill a hole through the center as marked. There are no numbers but as the hands move the time position is indicated.

Note   The system invented by Gord Armstrong has many applications. It can be used for inlays in furniture or floors. It allows even a novice woodworker to create wonderful works of inlay without the years of practice that would be necessary with traditional methods. Gord has made spiral inlays for lazy susans that are amazing. Very intricate inlays for gameboards like checkers or backgammon are easy with this system.

12

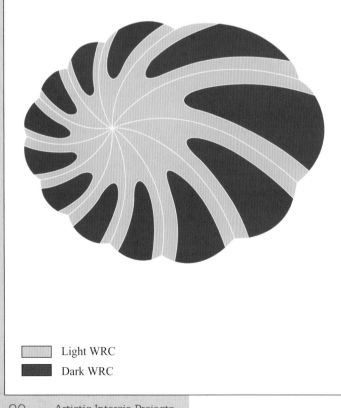

[legend square] Light WRC
[legend square] Dark WRC

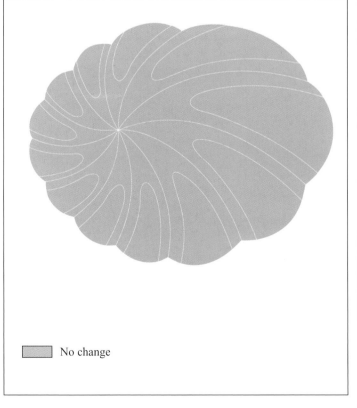

[legend square] No change

Pattern 50% original size

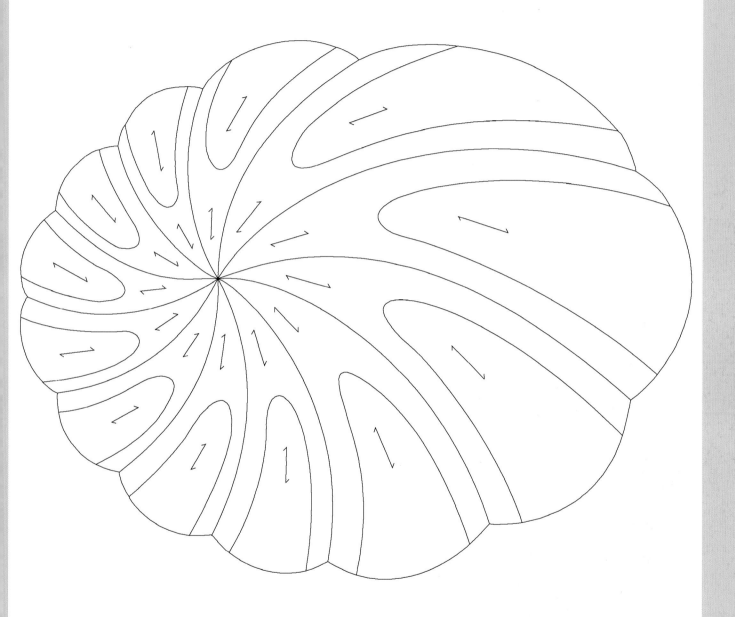

↦ direction of wood grain

⇢ slope down to this point

0 indicates open space

Rose Decoration

Rose Decoration

This simple intarsia rose can be used by itself or to enhance other projects; for example, a small commercial wooden box or a cabinet door. The finished rose is glued onto the box or door to make a special decoration. The rose can also be made as a stand alone intarsia project. There are many other ways that an intarsia decoration can be incorporated into other projects. In this project the top of the box is 8 ½ in x 5 ½ in, the corner bracket is 4 ½ in x 4 ½ in x ¼ in thick. I used the same size for the cupboard door.

No. of pieces   23
Finished size   4 ½ in x 3 ½ in x ³/₈ in

Wood needed	Quantities
Rose	
Chakte kok or bloodwood or aromatic cedar	2 in x 10 in
Poplar or sumac	1 in x 2 in
Light WRC	1 in x 4 in
Dark WRC	1 in x 1 in
Corner bracket	
Pau amarillo	6 in x 6 in x ¼ in thick

Directions

1   Size the rose pattern to fit onto the project of your choice. The top of the box that I used is 8 ½ in x 5 ¼ in (photo 1) .

2   I used aromatic cedar ³/₈ in thick for the rose on the box and aspen for the rose on the door, also ³/₈ in thick (photo 2).

3   Transfer (p4) the pattern (p85) to the wood using the method you prefer (p4).

4   Cut out carefully with a scroll saw and #3 blade. There are a number of small pieces so I used a double tooth blade for extra control (photo 3).

5   Assemble the cut out pieces and check for fit. Small projects with small pieces can be a challenge to fit. A false top (photo 4) for your scroll saw with a smaller blade hole can be helpful. See the section on fitting for tips on fitting the project (p9).

6   Raise and lower the pieces as the pattern suggests (p12).

7   Reassemble the pieces and mark the reference lines (p13) to help with the shaping. I kept the shaping fairly simple . The corner

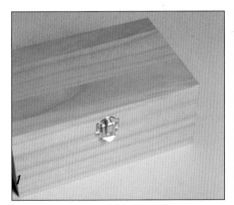

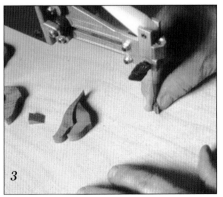

bracket has no shaping, you just sand the edges.

8   Sand the pieces to 220 grit.

9   Since the rose will be glued onto the box or door I didn't use a backing board. Assemble the rose in place and start the glue-up. Use an ordinary carpenter's glue.

10   When the glue has dried apply the finish (p18). Apply 3 coats and sand between coats. To keep the aspen white, finish it with a water base clear finish before finishing the rest of the project. **Note**   A white rose can be made from aspen.

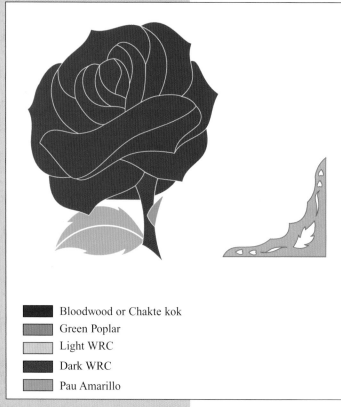

▨	Bloodwood or Chakte kok
▨	Green Poplar
▨	Light WRC
▨	Dark WRC
▨	Pau Amarillo

▨	L Lower ⅛ in
▨	No change

Pattern 60% original size

→ direction of wood grain

⇢▸ slope down to this point

0 indicates open space

Arctic Scene

Arctic Scene

This simple Arctic scene includes a polar bear, Inukshuk, and some mountains in the background. Inukshuks are a fascinating part of Inuit culture. They act in the capacity of a human being. They are made of stone and placed on the barren Arctic landscape. Their practical function is to aid navigation and hunting. But they also serve as reference points, food caches, and message centers. Spiritually they represent the people who survive the harsh land in traditional ways.

No. of pieces	19
Finished size	Polar bear 6 in x 3 $\frac{1}{2}$ in
	Inukshuk 3 $\frac{1}{2}$ in x 3 $\frac{3}{4}$ in
	Mountains 16 in x 1 1/2 in

Wood needed	Quantities
Aspen	6 in x 16 in x $\frac{7}{8}$ in thick

Directions

1   This project features slat backing. The number of slats you will need depends on the size of the project. You can use boards made from tree limbs such as caragana, aromatic cedar, sumac, apple, or diamond willow. Saw them into small boards 2 to 3 in wide. Attach them together with some slats across the back. See photos 1, 2, 3.

2   Most Inukshuk's are made from white stone but I wanted a different look. I chose aspen and began with $\frac{3}{8}$ in material.

3   Transfer (p4) the pattern (p89) to the wood with whichever method you prefer (p4).

4   Cut out the pieces carefully. I used a #3 DT/R style blade, but use whatever blade is suitable for the thickness of the material (photo 4).

5   Assemble the pieces and check for fit. The fitting of this project is fairly easy because the pieces fit at random on the slatted back.

6   Raise and lower (p12) any pieces the pattern suggests. This gives perspective to the scene (photo 5).

7   Shape the pieces to look as realistic as possible. I tried to make the Inukshuk rocks look rough and the bear's coat smooth. The mountains have the edges softened by sanding lightly.

8   Sand the pieces to 220 grit. Sand carefully on the fragile mountain pieces.

9   Assemble the pieces on the slat backing and adjust them until you like the placement.

Glue them in place with carpenter's glue.

10 Apply finish (p18) at this time. I chose to finish the slat back separately with a polyurethane finish and the white parts with a clear water base finish to keep them white.

11 Attach a hanger (p18).

Note This project offers a lot of creative latitude. No two projects will ever look the same depending on the wood you choose. Some woods such as caragana produce very unusual effects. Diamond willow is another good choice. The Inuksuk and the mountains could be made from various shades, but the polar bear has to be white.

☐ White Aspen

■ R Raise $^{1}/_{8}$ in   ■ L Lower $^{1}/_{8}$ in
■ No Change

Pattern 45% original size

→ direction of wood grain

⇢ slope down to this point

0 indicates open space

Batter Up Clock

Batter Up Clock

This fun project is suitable for any recreation room or child's bedroom. It functions as a wall decoration, a clock, and a place to hang a ball, glove, hat, bat, and ball. It's truly a multi-functional intarsia piece (photo 1). The design is straightforward and this project is fairly easy with only some slight variations. I burned in the stitches on the glove and baseballs.

No. of pieces   33
Finished size   21 in x 16 in

Wood needed	Quantities
Yellow cedar	4 in x 8 in
Pau amarillo	1 in x 2 in
Padauk	4 in x 6 in
Baltic birch plywood	$^1/_2$ in x 12 in x 14 in
Dark WRC	3 in x 6 in
Light WRC	6 in x 10 in
Aspen	4 in x 10 in

Directions

1   Enlarge (p4) the pattern (p93) to the desired size. Consult the formula on p4 for suggestions on how to enlarge the pattern to the same size as the original.
2   Choose the woods you want to use. Consult the pattern for some suggestions. Begin with $^3/_4$ in material. I used baltic birch plywood for the base. If you have a wide board of birch or basswood, you could use solid material.
3   Transfer the pattern to the wood using whichever method you prefer (p4).
4   A scroll saw is the best tool for cutting this project. A #7 P/S style blade works well. See the section on cutting tools (p6) for some other suggestions. Make sure the blade is square to the table. Cut carefully on the line.
5   The glove and hat are the only hard parts to fit on this project. Begin fitting the glove, then the hat. The rest is straightforward. When all the pieces are cut out assemble them according to the pattern and check for fit. The pieces should fit reasonably but don't need to be airtight. See the section on fitting (p9) for some suggestions.
6   When the pieces are fitted, raise and lower any pieces the pattern suggests. This adds perspective (photo 2).
7   Reassemble the project and mark on reference lines to assist with shaping. The base has only the edges shaped. Everyone is familiar with the baseball hat and glove so shape them as you know them. Try to give the hat and glove a rounded realistic look The more you shape the better it will look.
8   Sand each piece to 220 grit
9   Once the sanding is finished, consider backing board. Assemble the pieces on the backing board material and trace around them. Remove them and cut out the back.

3

10 Glue the pieces onto the backing board with carpenter's glue. Every project is different and there is no one way to do the glue-up. I usually set all the pieces on the backboard and then start the glue-up. With this project I glued the hat and glove down first and then the rest.

11 Drill holes for the 6 pegs which are 2 in long. If you prefer, $^3/_8$ in dowels work well. See photo 2).

12 The small baseballs that represent the hours on the clock are made from the ends of light colored dowel. Round the ends of the dowels and cut them off. You should have four 1 $^1/_4$ in diameter and eight $^3/_4$ in diameter baseballs. Burn the stitches or draw them in with a fine-tipped black marker (photo 3). The stitches on the glove are also burned (photo 4). The laces are actual leather shoe lace, cut to length and glued in place (photo 5).

13 Drill the hole in the back for the clock movement with a large Forstner bit or rout it out. I used an ordinary plastic style clock movement (photo 6).

14 Apply the finish of your choice. To keep the baseballs as white as possible finish them separately with a clear water base finish and glue them on later.

15 Attach a hanger (p18).

4

5

6

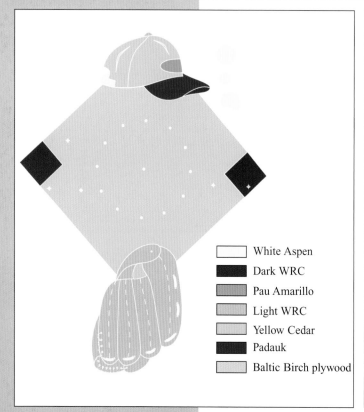

	White Aspen
	Dark WRC
	Pau Amarillo
	Light WRC
	Yellow Cedar
	Padauk
	Baltic Birch plywood

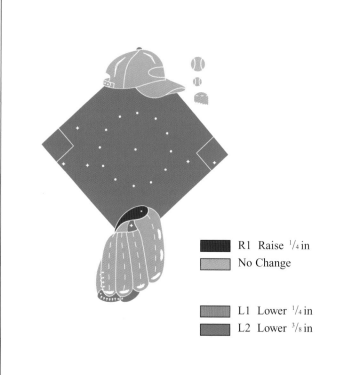

	R1 Raise $^1/_4$ in
	No Change
	L1 Lower $^1/_4$ in
	L2 Lower $^3/_8$ in

Pattern 40% original size

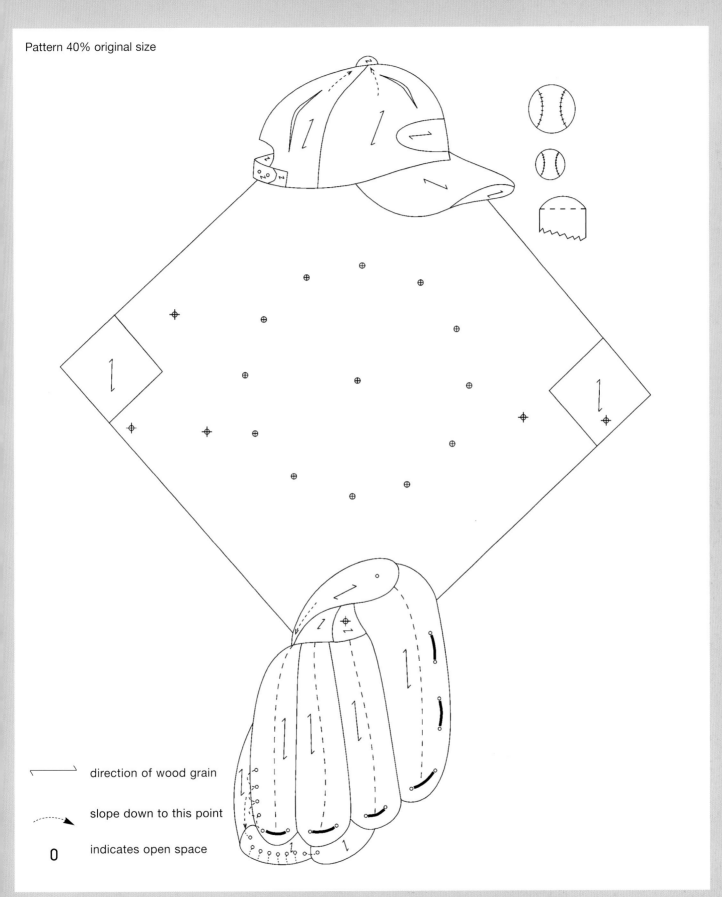

direction of wood grain

slope down to this point

0   indicates open space

Tiger

Tiger

This project has nine different levels of raising and lowering which makes it very difficult but the end result is well worth the extra effort. The project requires much shaping to give the tiger its life-like lines. This is a beautiful piece. Anyone who makes this project the actual size in this book will have their picture posted on my web site.

No. of pieces   80
Finished size   15 in x 12 in

Wood needed	Quantities
Black walnut	4 in x 16 in
Aspen	4 in x 16 in
Bloodwood	2 in x 4 in
Pau amarillo	2 in x 2 in
Light WRC or alder	4 in x 16 in
Medium WRC or mahogany	3 in x 6 in

Directions

1   Enlarge (p4) the pattern (p97) to the original size. A formula on p4 will show you how to do this.

2   Choose the woods using the pattern as a guide. Choose carefully to get the maximum artistic effect. Begin with ³/₄ in thick material.

3   Transfer (p4) the pattern to the wood with the method you prefer.

4   Cut out the pieces carefully. Refer to p6 for suggestions on blades. Cut on the line. However, if you have a steady hand with a scroll saw try cutting just inside the line for a better fit.

5   This is one of the hardest projects to fit that I have designed. Cut very carefully and keep a sharp blade in your saw at all times. The order in which you fit the pieces is up to you. If you are an experienced intarsia artist you will likely be able to plan your own order of attack. The following suggestions may help a novice decide where to start. The forehead and neck area are the most difficult. I fit the forehead area first, then the nose. I fitted the neck area separately and then fitted it to the head. Some of the pieces are quite delicate when cut out so be aware of that potential problem. Take

your time and with patience you can get a good fit. When you do you can be proud of a job well done. When you have all the pieces cut out assemble them and check for fit. Refer to p9 for fitting tips to get a tight fit.

6   With the pieces fitted, raise and lower any pieces the pattern suggests. The raising and lowering (p12) gives the project perspective. The parts closest to you will be the thickest and pieces farther away the thinnest (photo 1).

7   Reassemble the project and mark reference lines

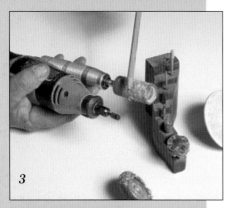

3

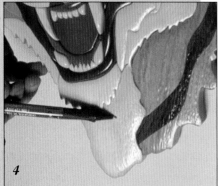

4

to help with the shaping. The shaping is extremely important so refer to the section on shaping for tips (p13).Take special pains to get the nose sloped back nicely to the forehead. Cut lines above Tiger's nose with a scroll saw. This will enhance the perspective of the project. The chin should drop sharply to the chest area and this will also emphasize the nose. The neck area should slope away to add more perspective. Take care with the eyes. The eyes can have an impact on how the project will look. I sometimes make a few different pairs and try them in the project to see which looks the best. Sometimes looking straight ahead is best and other times having the eyes looking off to the side adds a different dimension to the project.

8   Once you have the pieces shaped, sand all the pieces to 220 grit. Texturing some of the pieces will add to the realism of the project (photo 2). Photo 3 shows texturing tool and bits. Photo 4 shows close-up texturing technique for hair-like appearance.

9   This project can be made with or without a backing . See the section on backing (p16) for discussion of the two techniques. If you choose to finish without a backing it's easier to write the species of wood on the back of each wood. Many people appreciate this information (photo 5).

10   Apply the finish (p18) of your choice. I used 3 coats on the front and one on the back.

11   Attach a hanger (p18).

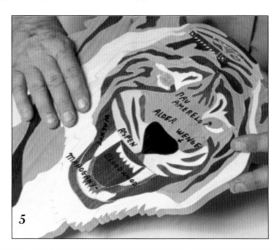

5

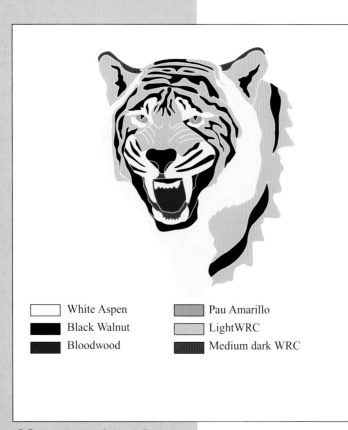

☐	White Aspen	▧	Pau Amarillo
■	Black Walnut	▨	LightWRC
■	Bloodwood	▨	Medium dark WRC

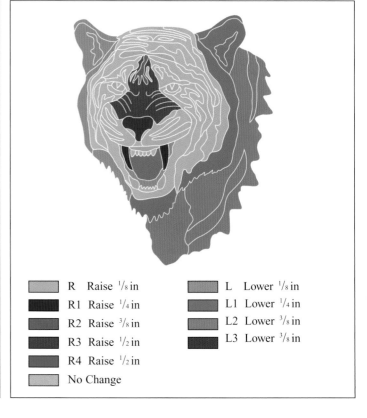

▨	R Raise $^1/_8$ in		▨	L Lower $^1/_8$ in
■	R1 Raise $^1/_4$ in		▨	L1 Lower $^1/_4$ in
▨	R2 Raise $^3/_8$ in		▨	L2 Lower $^3/_8$ in
▨	R3 Raise $^1/_2$ in		■	L3 Lower $^3/_8$ in
▨	R4 Raise $^1/_2$ in			
☐	No Change			

Pattern 55% original size

direction of wood grain

slope down to this point

0   indicates open space

Girl and Pony

Girl and Pony

This attractive project is suitable for any little girl's room. It's not too difficult and it provides the intarsia artist an opportunity to work with hardwoods for a very interesting finished effect. I used wood burning and texturing to add realism to the project.

No. of pieces   70
Finished size   18 in x 18 in

Wood needed	Quantities
Mahogany	6 in x 12 in
Alder	6 in x 12 in
Black cherry	4 in x 8 in
Bloodwood	2 in x 2 in
Pau amarillo	4 in x 8 in
Aspen	4 in x 6 in
Black walnut	2 in x 4 in
Poplar or Sumac	2 in x 8 in
Light WRC	2 in x 2 in
Medium WRC	2 in x 2 in
Dark WRC	4 in x 4 in

Directions

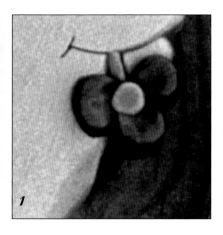

1

1   Enlarge (p4) the pattern (p102) to the original size or a size you prefer.

2   Choose the woods for the project. I used a number of hardwoods but you can work with whatever you like. Hardwoods provide a nicer finish and give the project a more polished look. Select the woods carefully and begin with ³/₄ in thick material.

3   Transfer (p4) the pattern to the wood with whichever technique you like.

4   This project incorporates some hardwoods which I believe add richness to a project. However, they are harder to cut. Keep your blade tight and replace it as soon as it shows signs of getting dull. Cut out the pieces with a scroll saw. Refer to p6 for tips and suggestions on blade style and size. Make sure your blade is square to the table. Cut right on the line. If you are an experienced scroller try cutting just inside the line for a better fit.

5   The most difficult part of this project is the flower in the pony's mouth (photo 1). You will need a scroll table with a small insert hole or make a false top with a small insert hole. The small pieces will have to be fitted and shaped by hand. Assemble the cut out pieces and check for

2

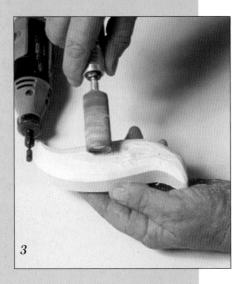

3

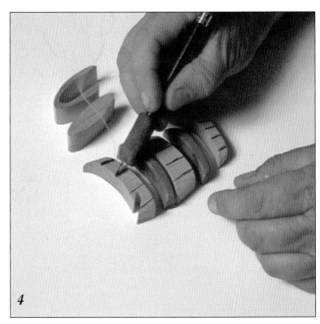

4

fit. See p9 for hints on fitting. As long as you are within the thickness of a credit card you will be fine. See p11.

6   Raise and lower (p12) (photo 2, p99) pieces as the pattern suggests to give perspective.

7   Reassemble the pieces and mark on reference lines (p13). These lines will help with the shaping.

8   Shape the pieces to achieve the appearance of a relief carving. A smooth transition from one level to the next is important. The more shaping the better the project will look. Some texturing is required on this project. The pony's mane and tail are textured to give the look of hair (photo 3).

9   Sand the pieces to at least 220 grit. You can do more if you wish.

10   I made the bucket from 6 pieces and I burned in lines in the wood (photo 4). The dots in the apron are ¼ in black walnut dowel (photo 5). The small dots in the shoes, are put in with a sharpened white dowel and cut off to length. This is an easy way to fit any size hole (photo 5). The dots in the sleeves are put in the same way (photo 6, p 101).

11   I used a backing board for this project but it can be made without if you prefer. Assemble the project on the backing board of ¼ in plywood. Trace around it and cut out the backing.

12   Reassemble the pieces on the backing and begin the glue-up. Use an ordinary white carpenter's glue.

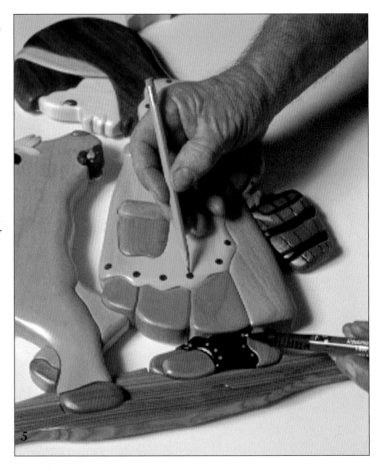

5

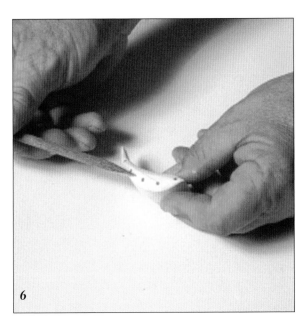

13 Once the glue has dried, round off the back edge.

14 Apply the finish (p18). Use at least 3 coats on the front and one on the back, sanding between coats.

15 Attach a hanger (p18).

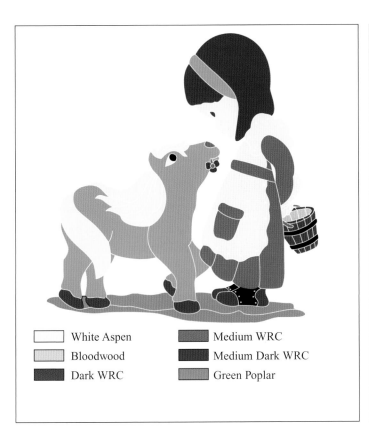

	White Aspen		Medium WRC
	Bloodwood		Medium Dark WRC
	Dark WRC		Green Poplar

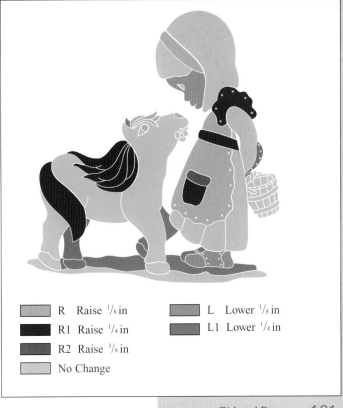

	R Raise $^{1}/_{8}$ in		L Lower $^{1}/_{8}$ in
	R1 Raise $^{1}/_{4}$ in		L1 Lower $^{1}/_{4}$ in
	R2 Raise $^{3}/_{8}$ in		
	No Change		

Pattern 40% original size

→ direction of wood grain

⇢▶ slope down to this point

0 indicates open space

Puppy in a Basket

Puppy in a Basket

The hardwoods used in the construction of this project make it look richer and more polished. The finished project has great appeal. I have made this project from cedar which looks very nice but has a different character than the project made from hardwood. I used texturing to provide a realistic look to the basket and the puppy's ears.

No. of pieces   45
Finished size   12 in x 12 in

Wood needed	Quantities
Medium WRC or butternut	6 in x 16 in
Light WRC or alder	3 in x 6 in
Dark WRC or black walnut	5 in x 10 in
Medium dark WRC or mahogany	4 in x 6 in
Aspen	4 in x 14 in
Black walnut	2 in x 2 in
Bloodwood	1 in x 4 in
Pau amarillo	1 in x 1 in

Directions

1   Enlarge (p4) the pattern (p106) to the original size. A formula on p4 will show you how to enlarge the pattern to the original size.

2   Use the pattern suggestions to choose the woods. However, you may wish to vary the woods according to your own artistic desires. Begin with $^3/_4$ in thick material.

3   Transfer the pattern (p4) to the wood with whichever method you prefer.

4   Cut out the pieces carefully, referring to p6 for suggestions on blades. Make sure your blade is square to the table. If you use a template, try cutting just inside the line for a better fit. You will need a steady hand.

5   When the pieces are cut out, assemble the project and check for fit. Pieces should fit well but need not be airtight. If the space is within the width of a credit card it won't be noticeable after shaping.

6   When you have the pieces fitted, raise and lower (p12) any pieces the pattern suggests. Raising and lowering (photo 1) add perspective to the project.

7   Reassemble the project and mark on reference lines (p13) to help with the shaping.

8   Carefully shape the pieces to achieve the look of relief carving. Pay special attention to the basket . Give the strips on the basket a wavy look (photo 2). Texture the puppy's ears and try to give them a wavy look (photo 3).

9   Sand the pieces smooth to 220 grit. You may sand to a finer grit if you choose. If you are using a paste type finish apply it now.

10   This project can be made with or without a

1

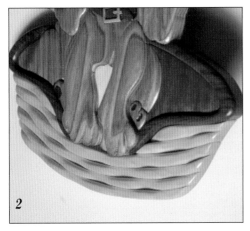

2

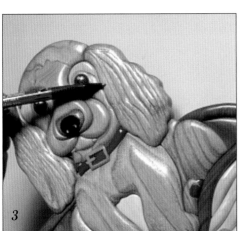

3

backing. See the section on backing (p16) for a description of the two techniques. Photo 4 has no backing which allows you to write the names of the woods used on the back of the project for easy reference for the project owner.

11 Once the project is glued up and the glue has dried, apply the finish. I use 3 coats to the front and one to the back, sanding between coats.

12 Attach the hanger (p18). Also see photo 4 (top of puppy's head).

4

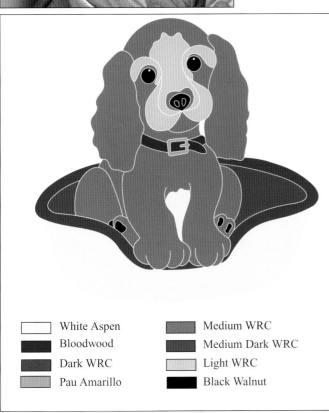

	White Aspen		Medium WRC
	Bloodwood		Medium Dark WRC
	Dark WRC		Light WRC
	Pau Amarillo		Black Walnut

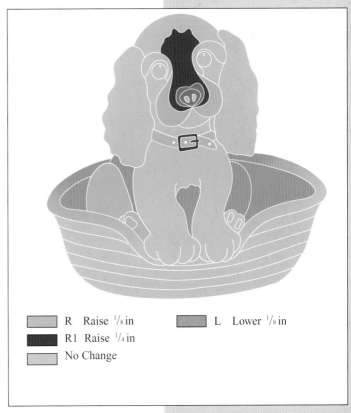

	R Raise ⅛ in		L Lower ⅛ in
	R1 Raise ¼ in		
	No Change		

Pattern 60% original size

⟶ direction of wood grain

⇢▶ slope down to this point

0 indicates open space

Fat Bike

Fat Bike

This is my version of a generic abstract bike. It's not supposed to represent any particular model. The fat bike looks very appealing with lots of raising and shaping to add to the contours. I used carving and wood burning for a detailed effect. This project is quite difficult.

No. of pieces   104
Finished size   28 in x 14 in

Wood needed	Quantities
Black walnut	4 in x 16 in
Bloodwood	4 in x 10 in
Pau amarillo	3 in x 10 in
Aspen	4 in x 12 in
Light WRC or alder	3 in x 4 in
Medium WRC or butternut	2 in x 4 in
Medium dark WRC or mahogany	2 in x 4 in

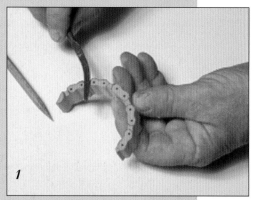

Directions

1   Enlarge the pattern (p111) to the original size using the formula on p4. I made it fairly large but you could make it a bit smaller if you wish.
2   Choose the wood (p5) for the project. Your choice reflects your artistic vision so this step is very important. Begin with ³/₄ in thick material.
3   Transfer the pattern to the wood with the technique you prefer (p4).
4   Cut out the pieces with a scroll saw. Make sure the blade is square to the table. A #7 double tooth or P/S tooth blade is a good choice. **Note** I have tried using a #3 hook tooth blade which gives the same cutting rate and a smaller kerf. New scrollers should cut on the line, more experienced cutters can try cutting just inside the line for a better fit. Cut the bike chain (photo 1) and front spring (photo 2) as one piece. Carve in chain links and spring lines.
5   This is a difficult project to fit because of the many small pieces. Fit the motor area first, then the back wheel. Once you have those two areas fit the rest shouldn't be too difficult. Change your blade often as you cut. A sharp blade cuts

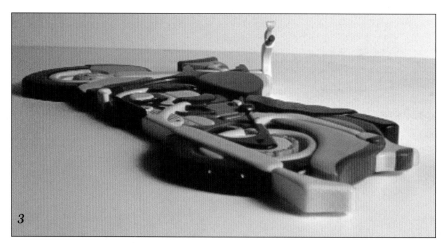

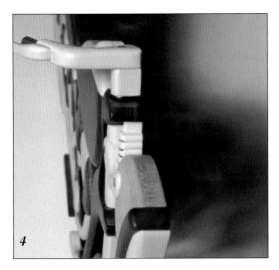

4

more accurately and you are less likely to force the blade off the line. Assemble the project and check for fit. See the section on fitting (p9) for tips and suggestions on how tightly the pieces should fit.

6   Raise and lower (p12) any pieces the pattern suggests. The more pieces you raise and lower the more perspective the project will have and the more abstract it will look (photo 3, p 108).

7   Try to give the larger pieces a fat rounded look. My design is an abstract bike, but it has the look of an old 45 Harley.

5

Have some fun with the shaping and let your imagination be your guide. Assemble the project and mark on the reference lines (p13) to help with the shaping. Shape the pieces to your liking. Carve the chain links with a sharp knife and a file. The pins in the links (photo 1, p 108) can be burned in or sharpen the end of ¼ in black walnut dowel (in photo). Glue the point in and cut it off flush. This technique works very well wherever you need a small colored dowel. Carve the front spring the same way shown in photos 2 & 4.

8   Sand all the pieces. I don't sand past 220 grit mainly to reduce the amount of dust I create.

9   Assemble the project on the cut out backing material and start the glue-up. Because this project is so long it is a good idea to clamp the ends down. A long project can twist as the glue dries. You could use a thicker backing, but that creates problems with backing the small pieces and rounding the back. Place it across the corner of a table or bench so you can clamp the ends down while you continue the glue-up. This isn't the best project for no backing but it can work if you want a free-standing project. See the section on backing (p16) for a discussion on backing methods and choose the technique you prefer. **Note**   This project can be made to hang on the wall or freestanding with a kick stand. I marked the pattern to show where to

6

drill the hole for the kick stand (photo 5)

10   Assemble the headlight using walnut dowels for the pins (photo 6).

11   Assemble the handlebars for the free-standing bike (photo 7, p 110)

12   Apply the finish of your choice. Use 3 coats on the front and

one on the back, sanding between coats.

13 Use half handle bars for hanging, (photo 6) and full handle bars for free standing (photo 7).

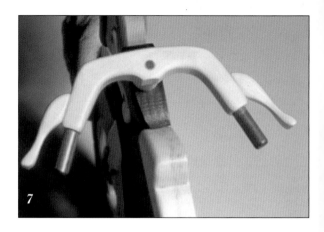

7

	White Aspen
	Black Walnut
	Pau Amarillo
	Medium Dark WRC
	Medium WRC
	Light WRC
	Bloodwood

	R Raise $^1/_8$ in
	R1 Raise $^1/_4$ in
	R2 Raise $^3/_8$ in
	No Change

| | L   Lower $^1/_8$ in |
| | L1 Lower $^1/_4$ in |

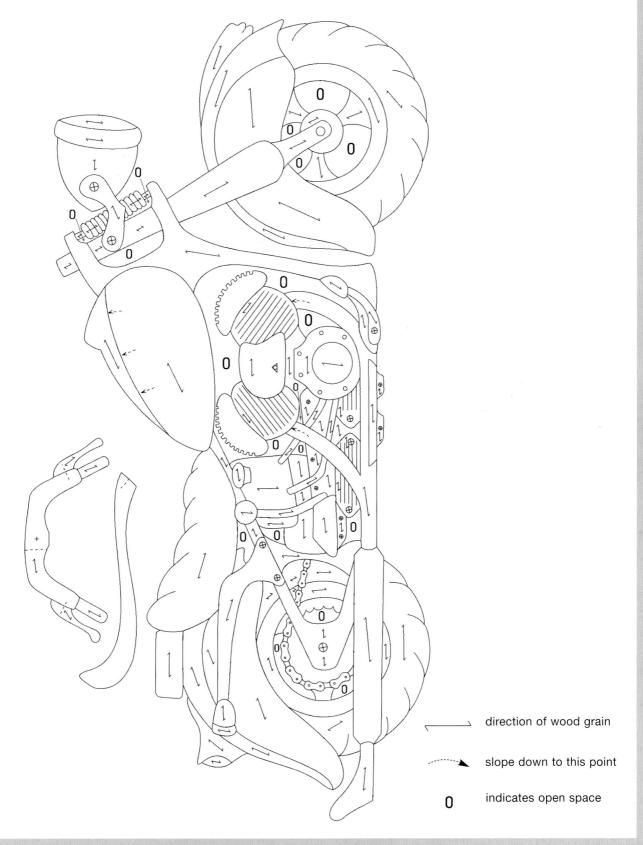

direction of wood grain

slope down to this point

0   indicates open space

Lighthouse and Quilt

Lighthouse and Quilt

This very different project combines the talents of two crafters – often a husband and wife team. The woodworking part is a fairly easy intarsia project. I searched for some hard-to-find blue/gray pine for this project to give it a characteristic weathered look. The quilting part is done in a stained glass technique. My wife and I collaborated on this project and we both recieved a lot of compliments.

No. of pieces	21		
Finished size	Lighthouse	12 1/4 in x 16 1/2 in
	Quilt	16 in x 22 in

Wood needed	Quantites
Bloodwood	5 in x 8 in
Pau amarillo	7 in x 24 in
Aspen	6 in x 12 in
Verawood or green poplar	4 in x 6 in
Medium WRC	4 in x 12 1/2 in
Dark WRC	1 in x 2 in
Pine	8 1/4 in x 12 in
Black walnut	4 in x 8 in

Fabric needed	Quantities
Black	16 in x 22 in
Red	6 in x 8 in
White	6 in x 12 in
Green	6 in x 10 in
Brown	4 in x 16 in
Dark brown	2 in x 4 in
Yellow	12 in x 16 in

Intarsia Directions

1 Enlarge (p4) the pattern (p116) to the original size or a size that you prefer, but remember that it has to coordinate with the quilt part of the project.
2 Choose the woods that the pattern suggests or other woods (p5) that will coordinate with the quilt. Begin with 3/4 in thick material.
3 Transfer the pattern to the wood with whichever method you prefer (p4).

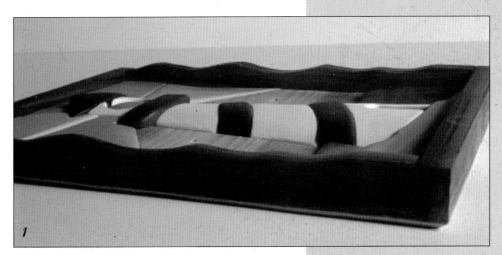
1

Intarsia wood design

4 Cut out the pieces carefully. Refer to pp6,7 for suggestions on cutting and blade choices. Make sure your blade is square to the table.

5 When the pieces are cut out assemble them and check for fit. Refer to the section on fitting (p9) for suggestions on how tight the pieces should fit and hints on how to improve the fit.

6 Once the pieces are fitted to your liking raise and lower (p12) any pieces the pattern suggests. See the different heights that gives perspective (photo 1).

7 Reassemble the pieces and mark on the reference lines (p13) to assist with the shaping. Try to achieve a smooth transition from one level to the next.

8 Sand all the pieces to at least 220 grit, or smoother if you wish.

9 Assemble the project on the backing material (p16). Leave 2 in around the outside for the frame. Make the frame any way you like and glue the entire project onto the backing board

10 When the glue has dried (at least one hour), round the back edge.

11 Apply the finish (p18) of your choice. Use 3 coats on the front and one on the back. Sand between coats.

12 Attach a hanger (p18).

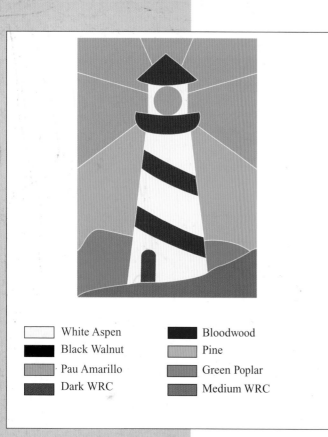

White Aspen		Bloodwood	
Black Walnut		Pine	
Pau Amarillo		Green Poplar	
Dark WRC		Medium WRC	

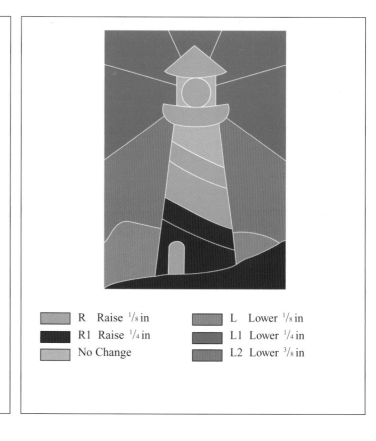

R Raise ¹/₈ in		L Lower ¹/₈ in	
R1 Raise ¹/₄ in		L1 Lower ¹/₄ in	
No Change		L2 Lower ³/₈ in	

Stained Glass Quilting Directions

1 Using a marking pen, trace the pattern (p117) onto freezer paper with the waxed or plastic side down.

2 Cut out the pattern with an x-acto or utility knife. When you are finished, the pattern will look like a web and this will be the template for the black leading that surrounds the various colored fabric pieces that makes the stained glass look. See quilt photo at below.

3 Prepare the foundation fabric. I used black. Make sure it's at least a inch larger than the pattern on all sides.

4 Lay the template on the fabric with the wax or plastic side down. Use a hot iron and with an up and down motion iron on the template. Turn the fabric over and press the other side.

5 Lay the fabric down with the template side facing up. Using a small pair of pointed scissors, pierce the center of the designs and cut them out. Leave the black leading about $1/4$ in from the template. This extra material is the seam allowance which will be folded and glued over. Clip all the curves towards the template. You don't have to clip the straight lines. Clip up to a couple threads from the template on the corners. You can cut out more than one design center at a time. Then attach the colored fabric. It's better to put in pieces as you go along so the project doesn't get out of shape.

6 Glue the folded parts with a fabric glue.

7 Cut the colored fabric pieces a bit larger than the space they are meant to fill. Glue them in place. The glue will hold them in place while you sew them.

8 Use black thread and set your machine to a fine zigzag. Set it so one thread hits the template (black leading) and the colored fabric (photo 1).

9 Finally, square up the project with a rotary cutter. Make a border any way you like. Layer the backing with the backing material you prefer. Quilt around all the colored shapes.

10 Attach a rod pocket (photo 2) with the binding material you prefer.

Stained glass quilt design

Pattern 50% original size

Intarsia Wood Pattern

direction of wood grain   ·····► slope down to this point   **0** indicates open space

Pattern 35% original size

Stained Glass Quilt Pattern

The intarsia and quilt project can be hung on the wall together

Piggy Bank

Piggy Bank

This intarsia piggy bank is my version of the old classic. It's a fun project with a bit of a challenge. Once finished it makes an attractive repository for small change or encourages small children to save their pennies.

No. of pieces   30
Finished size   10 in x 10 in

Wood needed	Quantites
Black walnut	2 in x 2 in
Aspen	4 in x 6 in
Aromatic cedar	2 in x 2 in
Padauk	2 in x 2 in
Light WRC	5 in x 12 in
Medium light WRC	3 in x 6 in
Dark WRC	6 in x 6 in
Birch or pine	1 piece 1 $^1/_2$ in thick 10 in x 10 in

Directions

1 The front part of the bank is ordinary intarsia. Enlarge the pattern (p123) to the size of the original (p4). You can make it smaller or larger if you wish.
2 Choose the woods (p5) for the project of your own selection or using my pattern suggestions. Pay special attention to wood shades and grain direction which greatly affect the finished look of the project. Begin with $^3/_4$ in thick material.
3 Transfer the pattern to the wood (p4) with whichever method you prefer.
4 Cut out the pieces with a scroll saw. Make sure the blade is square to the table. A #7 P/S or double tooth blade works well. Cut carefully on the line. If you have a steady hand with a scroll saw try cutting just inside the line for a better fit. Drill the pig's notstrils with $^1/_2$ in bit.
5 This project isn't too difficult to fit if you take your time. The eyes, nose, and mouth all fit inside the head, which can present some challenge. Cut out the head first, then fit the nose in place. Trace the eye area onto some white wood. Make the eyes and fit them into their space. Use the same technique with the mouth. Trace the mouth area onto the correct

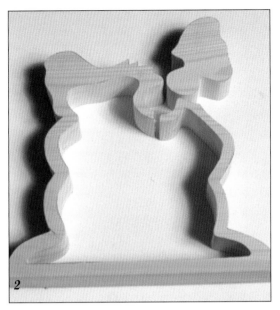

shade of wood. Assemble the project and check for fit. See p9 for hints on fitting and suggestions for how tight pieces should fit.

6   Once the fitting is complete, raise and lower (p12) any pieces the pattern suggests to give perspective (photo 1).

7   Reassemble the project and mark on the reference lines (p13). These will help with the shaping.

8   Round the pig's head as much as possible. The nose should be more flat on the front part and not sloped too much to the face. A pig's nose is long and prominent. Shape the pieces to achieve the appearance of relief carving. Aim for a smooth transition from one level to the next. The more shaping you do the better a project looks.

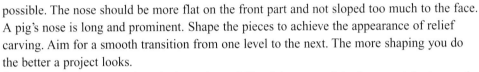

9   Sand the pieces smooth. I don't sand past 220 grit because of the increased dust caused by more sanding. But how much you sand is a matter of personal choice. If you are using a paste/gel type finish or a water base finish on the white areas apply it now.

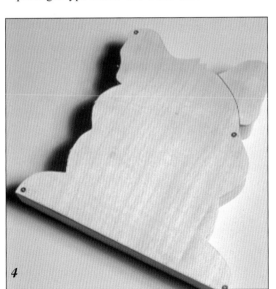

10   At this point the project becomes different from an ordinary intarsia project. Assemble the project onto the 1 $^1/_2$ in thick material you are using for the body. Trace around the project. Cut the bank body $^1/_8$ in smaller than the project.

11   Cut out the inside of the bank body as indicated on the pattern (photo 2). You will need a good blade to cut this thickness on a scroll saw. A #9 P/S or #5 H/T will handle the thickness. Take your time and allow the saw to work through the material. If you push the saw you will get a barrel cut. Take special care cutting out the removable ear. The cut must be square so the ear can be slid out of the body. The coins go in a slot in the ear space.

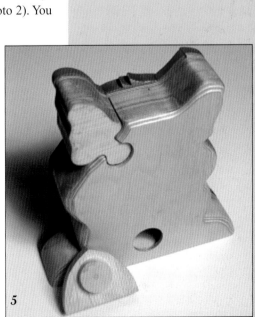

12   Make the front and back boards. Trace the body outline onto $^1/_4$ in plywood. Be careful that the slot doesn't spread while you are tracing. Put the ear in place and use a clamp to hold it while you are tracing (photo 3).

13   The front board is cut off as indicated by the dotted line. The back board

has the entire left ear cut out of it (photo 4). This allows the ear to be removed only from the back of the bank (photo 5).

14 Glue the front board onto the bank body with the left ear in place and clamped so it won't spread too much. I used ³/₄ in screws to hold the front board in place while the glue dried. Once dry, remove the screws. Glue the ear piece cut from the front board onto the ear.

15 Drill a 1¹/₂ in hole in the back board to remove the coins and then glue it onto the bank body. Make a hole plug as shown in photo 5 or purchase a plastic bank plug.

16 Now glue the intarsia pig face onto the front board. Make sure it's evenly spaced on the board.

17 Apply the finish of your choice (p18). Use 3 coats on the front and one on the back, sanding between coats.

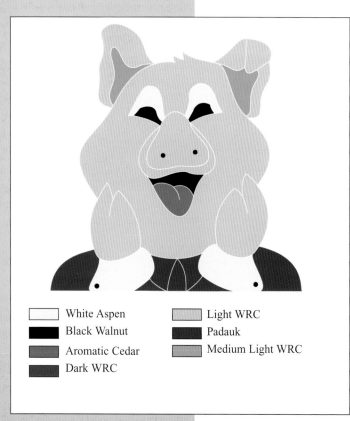

☐ White Aspen	☐ Light WRC
■ Black Walnut	■ Padauk
■ Aromatic Cedar	■ Medium Light WRC
■ Dark WRC	

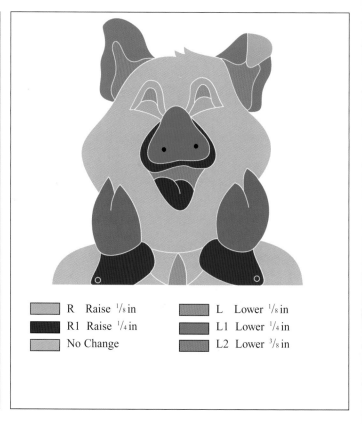

R Raise ¹/₈ in	L Lower ¹/₈ in
R1 Raise ¹/₄ in	L1 Lower ¹/₄ in
No Change	L2 Lower ³/₈ in

Pattern 75% original size

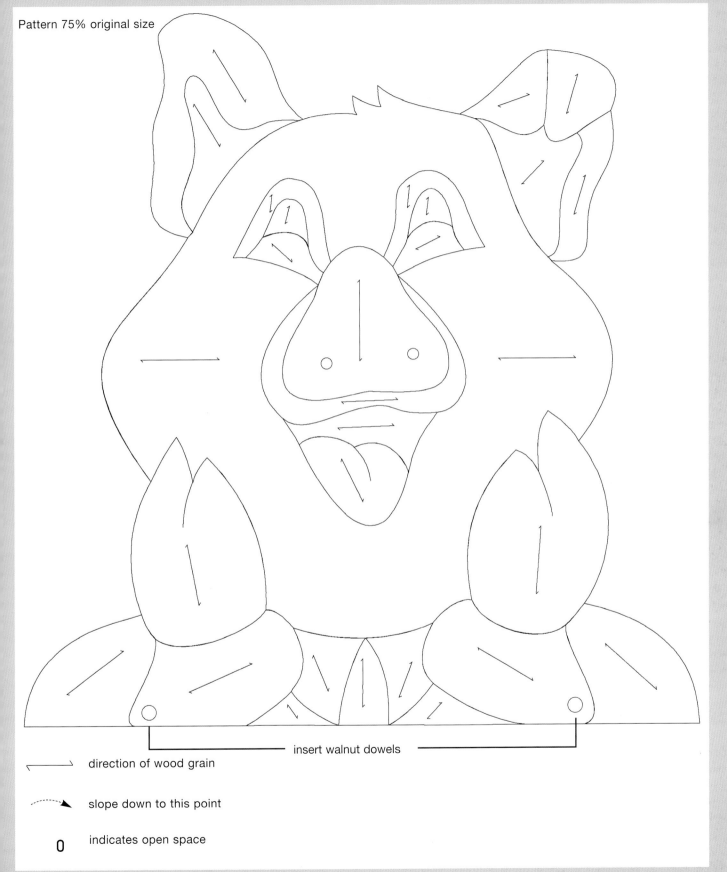

insert walnut dowels

↘ direction of wood grain

⟍▸ slope down to this point

0 indicates open space

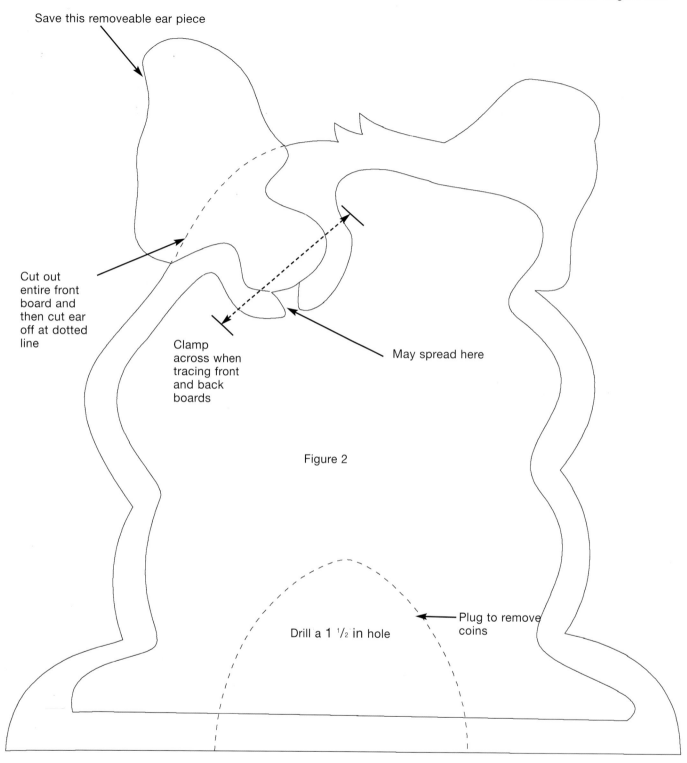

Save this removeable ear piece

Cut out
entire front
board and
then cut ear
off at dotted
line

Clamp
across when
tracing front
and back
boards

May spread here

Figure 2

Drill a 1 ½ in hole

Plug to remove
coins

Rear View